Getting Special Needs Kids Ready for the Real World

Getting Special Needs Kids Ready for the Real World

SPECIAL EDUCATION FROM A LOVE AND LOGIC PERSPECTIVE

David Funk

Library of Congress Cataloging-in-Publication Data

Funk, David, 1946-
    Getting special needs kids ready for the real world : special
    education from a love and logic perspective / [David Funk].
        p. cm.
    Includes bibliographical references and index.
    ISBN 1-930429-78-9 (alk. paper)
    1. Special education—United States. 2. Learning disabled
children—Education—United States. 3. Teacher-student
relationships—United States. I. Title.
LC3981.F888 2005
371.9—dc22
                                                                2005030797

Project Coordinator: Carol Thomas
Editing: Jason Cook, Denver, CO
Indexing: Douglas J. Easton, New West Indexing, Westminster, CO
Interior Design: Dianne Nelson, Shadow Canyon Graphics, Golden, CO
Cover Design: Meghan Dews

Published and printed in the United States of America.

This book is dedicated to my beloved wife, Diane, and my immediate and extended family. I also want to recognize the influence of Jim Fay. He has been a mentor and is responsible for my staying in education.

I also want to acknowledge my professional colleagues and all of the others who have contributed to what I have learned—especially the "therapy" lunch group and the guys who meet on Fridays at six for breakfast.

Contents

Preface

THIS BOOK IS WRITTEN WITH THE FULL UNDERSTANDING that educating kids is a continuing process. Amended legislation, expanding case law, medical discoveries, and educational technologies are significant influences that effect change. A maturity has developed in both regular and special education that provides a substantial understanding of how to teach almost anyone. To continue speculation about what to do with challenging students may provide a level of intellectual stimulation, but will certainly hamper us from serving them effectively. What is needed throughout our educational structure is an adherence to the fundamentals of learning and behavior.

Those fundamentals are encapsulated in the Four Key Principles of Love and Logic, a paradigm that was formulated during a drive with Jim Fay from Milwaukee to Madison (Wisconsin). In that ninety-mile trip we analyzed why Love and Logic is effective and applicable to a variety of situations faced by parents and teachers. The majority of the chapters in this book incorporate various nuances and applications of those basic principles.

Jim was a person who influenced me at a critical time in my career. He, too, had influences in his life that allowed him to develop into a master educator. My great hope is that the information presented here will be a worthy continuation of the work of those who have taught me. I am also reminded of the words written by the author of Ecclesiastes some millennia ago: "Of making many books, there is no end . . ." Regardless of what lofty spiritual meaning may have been intended, these words remind me that deciding when to stop writing is the hardest part. Where does one stop when the insights of so many teachers are yet to be recorded?

Chapter 1

The Essentials of Love and Logic

My goal is to present Love and Logic in such a way
that people can decide for themselves if it is right
for them, not so they will buy it.

— JIM FAY

Perhaps Not Made in Heaven,
but a Match Nevertheless

MY FIRST EXPOSURE TO LOVE AND LOGIC was one of caution. I had been teaching special education students for several years and had dealt with some fairly tough kids who didn't really want to learn what school had to offer. Furthermore, these kids seemed to gain great satisfaction from purposely breaking rules. Any program with "love" in it, I reasoned, was probably a tad soft on kids who needed shaping up.

However, the honest fact is that I was running into some problems trying to control kids' behavior by overpowering or manipulating them into behaving my way. When I first considered Love and Logic, I surely wasn't convinced this new way (new for me) of dealing with kids would work, but I needed to find some alternatives to what wasn't working well for me. And then there was the issue that I couldn't devise any valid argument to contradict Love and Logic's basic concepts.

Another problem posed an even greater risk for me: Every time I tried an idea, it worked. This was kind of annoying, really, because the theory was so commonsense that I was chagrined I hadn't figured it out on my own. But what I did eventually catch on to was that Love and Logic gave a framework for teaching and was, in a way, educational theory translated into practical language.

Looking at Life Through Love and Logic

WHAT I CAME TO UNDERSTAND EARLY ON was that the premise of Love and Logic is fairly simple and forthright: Everyone's behavior is consistent with how they understand the world. This philosophy may seem a simple enough explanation, until we realize that there are about as many "understandings" as there are people—making relationships ripe for conflict and confusion. For instance, although I can always justify my own actions, surely, when others do "wrong" (i.e., things I don't like or agree with), they know the error of their ways and then go ahead and engage in inappropriate behavior anyway.

This was my basic orientation toward students for the first several years I taught. In fact, this is pretty much the way I thought about everybody, including my casual acquaintances, close friends, and even immediate family. It was somewhat of a "revelation" when I realized that just about everyone pretty much operated the same way I did. Finding people who believe that some action they are contemplating makes no sense and yet go ahead and do it anyway is truly a rare find.

I wish my penchant for believing that I was right and everyone else was wrong would have been a result of naiveté or even immaturity. It is somewhat awkward to realize that such a mind-set is more a matter of being egocentric. My only comfort was knowing I was "certifiably normal," because when there are differences of opinion, just about everyone believes they are in the right and others are almost always in the wrong.

Perception: The Foundation of Volitional Behavior

SOME YEARS AGO I HEARD AN ALTERATION of a common saying that chaos (rather than necessity) is the mother of invention. In an effort to provide ourselves with stability and security, our minds seem to have a singular purpose to form patterns to make sense of a world that would otherwise be quite confusing.

For instance, language involves sounds that have meaning sufficient to allow for communication between those with a common linguistic base. These patterns also incorporate word relationships, time references, and structured sequences—all of which are components that convey particular meaning. Anyone who has tried to learn a new language later in life knows that mastering vocabulary is difficult enough—it's the syntax, pronunciation, and innuendoes that are the really hard part.

Developing moral, political, or cultural values involves the process of developing patterns. Even views that a student develops about school follow much the same path. Although a number of individual variables such as experience, temperament, and circumstance go into developing our beliefs, once the pattern is set, we all have a very strong tendency to act consistent with that construct.

We have a similarly strong tendency to disregard, reinterpret, or even outright reject information to the contrary. If I hold to a particular notion and someone else doesn't, it is so very easy to discount their ideas. Some even go to the extreme of dehumanizing others who think differently. So it is not so much that our behavior is governed by what we think is right or wrong, as much as our behavior is governed by maintaining consistency with what we believe at the time.

Interrupting vs. Interjecting

We have all developed great skill in giving our own behavior a positive attribution, regardless of what others might think. I recall a situation that occurred during a presentation at a Headstart conference. In the middle of what I thought to be cogent comments dealing with this very topic of perception, a rather heavy-set school-bus driver quite boldly made a comment that kids know they are doing wrong because they "get guilty" right away—an observation that guilt comes after, rather than before, the action. But then another point was made relative to this man's comment: Some participants viewed it as a discourteous interruption and, as such, were a bit miffed. However, this was certainly not the way the man understood his own behavior. In his view, he had not interrupted. Rather, he had interjected a thought, and an important one at that. Even the man himself would probably have maintained that interrupting is bad, yet how could contributing a pertinent comment be anything but good? We are quite accomplished at understanding the intent of our own behavior. The real skill, however, is understanding the perspective of others.

Monkeys in the Classroom

I recall another incident that relates to how we understand the righteousness of our own perspective. In a presentation to an audience that included high school teachers, I mentioned that I had made a promise to myself early in my career to not kick kids out of my classroom. I further indicated that this decision had been based on a conclusion on my part (completely subjective) that to do so would give me the feeling I had lost control of my classroom—clear evidence of being an ineffective teacher. I went on to say that as my career progressed, although I had held true to the promise, I'd come to realize there were times it would have been better for me and better for the kid had I done some removal.

Even though I emphasized that I applied this "rule" to no one else, a fairly large, balding, near-retirement-aged "shop" teacher simultaneously raised his hand and said, "Are you saying kids shouldn't be kicked out of class?" Wanting to somewhat maintain the flow of the presentation, I indicated that, certainly, there are times that sending a kid to the office is proper, provided that this is not the only option for dealing with offensive behavior.

At the end of the presentation, this teacher approached me with confident words: "I want you to know, I don't let monkeys run my classroom." A very interesting choice of words for an unsolicited comment. I told him that I didn't want monkeys running the classroom either—but that perhaps we differed on just who we thought the monkeys were.

Duane and the Drywall Debacle

Perception is changed when information is taken into our cognitive system in a way that alters the pattern we had previously accepted. Virtually all of us have had the experience of saying something only to regret doing so when we come to see the situation differently. Our culture even has a phrase for such circumstances: "Putting one's foot in one's mouth." A family story comes to mind.

When my family gets together, old stories are retold and new ones are added to the compendium. We have a rich tradition of events, like when while swimming in the river behind my house, I tied two bleach bottles together and used them as floats to keep my brother, Duane, the next-to-youngest sibling, from going under. At the time, I had no clue that our mother's perspective about this might have been very different than mine. Whereas I thought of the device as a creative solution to keep my brother from sinking (and indeed, "water wings" did eventually became all the rage), Mom had heart palpitations and didn't breathe much until Duane got himself back on dry land.

Duane, like the rest of my family, has contributed much to our story-telling tradition. One story in particular stands out in my mind as exemplifying the concept that behavior is always consistent with per-ception. And that, when perception shifts, behavior changes are sure to follow.

To fully appreciate this story, you need to know a bit about my brother. He is a good man with a soft heart and a quick temper. He also has a strong opinion about every conceivable topic and is more than willing to "share" those opinions with anyone who might think contrarily.

To augment his income and occupy his time, Duane buys houses that have been damaged by fire (which can be bought pretty cheaply), fixes them up, and then sells or rents them. Obviously, there is a lot of work involved in restoring such buildings, and they need lots of dry-walling. Although Duane is skilled in remodeling, it takes him a long time to obtain the glass-smooth wall surface that professionals seem to achieve with ease.

On one particularly difficult job, Duane was using a drywall com-pound (the stuff used to smooth imperfections on the surface of a wall) that took 240 minutes to dry. Although four hours might seem to provide plenty of time for surface-smoothing, the material was setting faster than Duane could work it, so he decided to buy some compound that would give him a bit more working time.

He entered a supply store and asked for a specific type and brand of compound that took 300 minutes to dry. The clerk told Duane that the store was sold out and, in fact, was no longer planning to stock that particular item, because so few people ever requested such a slow-acting product. Perhaps my brother interpreted this remark as a nega-tive commentary on his drywalling skills, or maybe he was just per-turbed that he had been denied what he'd come for. At any rate, the stress hormones started oozing into his brain, causing a deterioration in his ability to think logically.

After Duane expressed his position about this managerial decision, the clerk mentioned that although the specific 300-minute product

Duane wanted wasn't available, the store did have a product, from a different manufacturer and generally used for finishing work, that set in five hours. In response, and with full confidence, my brother said, "I came here for 300-minute compound and I'm not buying any of this five-hour s- - -."

After my brother emphasized his point with additional verbiage, the clerk, looking a bit confused, asked, "But, sir, what is the difference?" At this point, my brother validated all of the research studies that conclude that high stress significantly restricts functioning of the frontal cortex, and therefore a person's capacity for rational thought. In a tone of voice reserved for pronouncements of absolute truth by the righteously indignant, he said, "Let me tell you, where I went to school, there was a lot of difference!" He then left, feeling satisfied that no young kid was going to pull anything over on him.

This satisfaction lasted throughout the day, and he looked forward to telling the story that night to Karen, his future wife, when he picked her up from work. No sooner had he finished his diatribe when Karen asked him, with a hint of puzzlement, about the difference between the drying times of the two products. As Duane inhaled deeply, with his index finger poised in preparation for a definitive explanation, he realized, in a blaze of horror, that there wasn't any difference at all.

In an attempt to heal his now injured ego (Karen, of course, despite being his significant other, would not be the source of such comfort), Duane called Mom. This, too, was counterproductive, and as he will tell you, the majority of that long-distance call was spent listening to Mom engaged in uncontrollable laughter. She did compose herself, however, just long enough to say a typical "momism": "Duane, you know what you should do."

Now, adding to the humiliation he had to suffer, there was guilt. Duane's perception changed and so did his behavior. We might wish he had taken the high road and gone back to the store to apologize. Instead, he never went back to that store again.

The Mutilated Ear and the Hugger

Sometimes perceptual confusion creates a funny story. However, there are other times when humor is not at all part of the outcome. Often, the characteristics of disabled kids create situations where even the professionals working with them believe dramatic measures are needed. Unfortunate situations arise when the interventions do not address the actual problem. The following story is extreme, but it is often in the extremes that we gain the proper perspective.

A man with significant developmental delays was repeatedly hitting his ear with the ball of his hand. So severe was this behavior that his ear was hardly recognizable. The presumption of the day was that self-mutilation was a common characteristic of mental retardation, and so no other explanation was deemed necessary. The logical conclusion was that, to offset this man's limited capacity, drastic measures were justified. As a result, aversive shock treatment was prescribed.

In actuality, there was a twofold problem. First, the electric shock treatment evidently didn't work very well. It continued over the course of seventeen years, even though the man kept hitting his ear with the same intensity and frequency. Second, as an eventual medical examination revealed, the original conclusion of why he kept hitting himself was well off the mark.

The real problem was that this man had an undetected episodic middle ear infection and a tooth abscess. Because of the way affected nerves were arranged, repeatedly hitting his ear caused a numbness that gave him some relief from the pain. Certainly, he had a limited intellectual capacity that affected his understanding and ability to communicate, but the man hit his ear because he was in pain, and no amount of aversive shock changed this. After the physical conditions were corrected, there was no record of him hitting his ear again.

No doubt that those who promulgated the prescribed shock therapy were sincere and maybe even felt that their fairly extreme intervention was the only thing available. The fact that it didn't work evidently didn't deter them from this act of faith. But they were wrong, very wrong.

Another story comes to mind that, although not as dramatic, nevertheless emphasizes the same lesson. A girl with cognitive issues was engaging in a behavior that, when she was young, was considered cute, but was viewed as quite inappropriate when she became a teenager. She was constantly hugging people. Staff, peers, or strangers, it didn't much seem to matter to her. She grabbed anyone and held them too tight for too long.

The staff at the residential school where she lived decided that enough was enough. Neither positive nor negative reinforcement worked, so something stronger seemed the only option. As with the man with the mutilated ear, this young lady lived at a time when aversive therapy had not yet received a lot of negative press, and preparation was made to consult an expert.

This expert had a remarkable protocol and was well ahead of his time. Whenever he was called in to develop a behavior intervention, he involved the "subjects" to the degree they were capable. Although this girl had some serious emotional and cognitive problems, she could still answer simple questions. One of the first asked of her by this new psychologist was, "Why do you hug people?"

Evidently, no one had ever asked her before, which was so sad for everyone involved, notwithstanding the girl herself. Her response, consistent with her developmental level, was nevertheless forthright and gave a major clue to developing an effective intervention. "Because I so cold," was her answer, which led to the solution: a couple of heavy, warm sweaters!

The point of these stories, and a foundational idea of Love and Logic, is that interpreting one person's behavior through another person's perception can result in needless confusion and ineffectiveness. In education, we simply don't have the luxury of justifying such inefficiencies.

The Survey

To a very large degree, students are declared problems on the basis of information filtered through the perceptions of those making decisions. The following is only a representative example of this not-rare phenomenon.

A sixth-grade student attending a local parochial school had been referred for a special education evaluation. As part of this assessment, a behavior rating scale using a forced-response format (with "never," "sometimes," "often," and "always" as the only options) was completed by his parents and teachers. Upon analysis, the responses of the school staff and the parents were so different that the psychologist opined the parents were in denial. Such a determination carried heavy implications and, as one can imagine, put the parents quite on the defensive. In reality, the problem was more one of perception than anything else.

This student was reported as having had police involvement, a theft record, and conflicted social interactions. Without any further investigation, it would seem reasonable to conclude that this kid had some significant behavior problems. However, the reality was that what seemed to be a life of crime was actually a single incident of pilfering some money from his youth activity group. He, of course, had faced some temporary social consequence and the police had been called in to "teach him a lesson." The student had exhibited such behavior neither before nor after, and the lone incident was certainly not indicative of a budding young delinquent.

The problem arose from an uncritical acceptance of the adult responses to an assessment questionnaire. In response to survey questions that referenced such behavior, the teachers indicated "sometimes." The father, however, viewed this circumstance as a single, isolated incident and interjected a "1" on the response form. "Never," he reasoned, would not be accurate, and neither would "sometimes," which clearly implies more than a single instance. However, "1" was not a scorable option and there was an accusation that the parents were not willing to come to grips with their son's emotional problems.

Another survey question asked whether the student had engaged in cheating. Indeed, earlier that year, for about two weeks, this boy had copied from a classmate's math homework. In all of the student's career, and ever since the cheating infraction, there had been no indication of other incidents. The parent viewed this as an isolated event in an almost seven-year school career and stated that none of the available responses would be an accurate indication of what had actually happened. In response, the father indicated "sometimes" as his answer.

The teachers, however, indicated "often," because as their representative charged, the behavior had occurred over the course of several days. In addition, the teachers wanted to emphasize their strong moral aversion to cheating and that this particular student's behavior was "far worse" than that of the others in his class. The teachers did not want this particular situation to be underestimated by diluting their response. As a result, the information they brought to the evaluation team was more a measure of their moral indignation than factual information about the kid's level of abnormal behavior.

A Foundation for Both Problems and Solutions

"Perception" stories might be interesting and even humorous if the potential for educational tragedy weren't so great. Deciding what to do with individual students depends very much on the decisions of teams of people who have highly individual perspectives. Likewise, there are a number of perspectives about proper instruction of students, appropriate social behavior, or even acceptable rates of skill acquisition. Unless there is a point of mutual agreement between those who are drafting the rules and others who are making educational interpretations, significant time and effort may be wasted.

Four Key Principles

WHEREAS PERCEPTION CAN BE CONSIDERED the foundation of human behavior, the Four Key Principles of Love and Logic constitute the superstructure. As with other areas of human endeavor, it is often necessary to have a paradigm to serve as a template for understanding and explaining given phenomena. Educational issues that focus on student performance are no exception.

The Four Key Principles of Love and Logic were developed from first observing and then analyzing why people do what they do. The result is an understanding that, although humans may well be the most complex of God's creations, a few basic principles explain most of volitional behavior. Just as most of matter is composed of a few primary components (electrons, neutrons, protons, and other subatomic particles), and even the most complex computers operate using what are essentially a bunch of on-off switches, a few basic concepts seem to govern human behavior:

1. *Self-concept:* Self-concept is the perception people have of themselves. The fact that our society associates high ability with high worth puts kids with any level of skill deficit at a disadvantage from the start. The components of self-concept include feelings of being valued, capable, and unique. When any of these elements are lacking or attacked, people attempt to defend what dignity they have left and engage in such "recovery" behavior as denial, macho-ness, clowning, or belligerence. Conversely, when people feel their personhood is not under attack, learning is easier and kids give teachers less hassle. An added benefit is that most of the problems kids have in school stem from self-concept issues. If this one area is addressed by teachers, they get a significant bang for their intervention buck.

2. *Shared control:* People don't like to be made to do things, even if they recognize their best interest may well be at risk if they don't. In the realm of education, control becomes a significant factor. Discipline, motivation, and anger management all involve issues of getting kids to do what they might not be inclined to bring about on their own. When people perceive that their rightful control over themselves is being taken away, power struggles ensue. The

inevitable result is that time and effort are expended to enforce a hierarchy of authority. This can take the form of passive-aggressive/passive-resistive behavior, overt aggression, or other conduct that sabotages the goal of the person in authority. Because the very nature of society requires some curtailing of individual behavior, a key to effectiveness in adult–child relationships is establishing limits without making the problem worse.

3. ***Empathy with consequence:*** Some of life's most important lessons are learned when we experience the logical consequences of our decisions rather than being artificially punished or rewarded for them. However, to learn from experience necessitates that people make a connection between what they do and what happens to them. The characteristic of some students is that they are unable to adequately comprehend cause/effect relationships.

   Students who lack this ability to make logical connections (i.e., perceive consequences) are quite oriented to attributing success and failure to luck and misfortune. Students often give up to avoid the hurt that comes from failure. They also give up because they have formed the belief that regardless of what they do in school, they have little direct influence on outcomes. For many kids, this feels a safer course, at least for the short term.

   When students are taught to learn from consequences, they also learn to "own" problems and thereby become invested in the solution. By arriving at the conclusion that there is a logical (albeit, subjective) connection between what they do and what happens to them, students form the cause/effect foundation for responsibility. The role of empathy is to validate the selfhood of the student so that the adult is never the direct source of the child's anger or hurting. Empathy acknowledges the student's feelings without condoning or excusing the behavior. In addition, empathy inhibits the student from developing an externalized locus of control and blaming others as a way to escape the discomfort that comes from making bad decisions.

4. ***Shared thinking:*** When dealing with students, we can usually get a lot more accomplished if they are in the thinking, rather than the emotional, state. A critical factor in dealing with people is understanding that all sensory information goes through the emotional centers of the brain first. Affective responses are very individual, but the universal principle is that the more stressed we become, the less we can invoke rational thought.

    Students, especially those who have problems in school, are often on alert, because their innate conditions affect their performance and relationships. When teachers interact with students in such a way that thinking rather than reacting is taking place, instruction is much more easily accomplished. The more thinking students do, the more investment and ownership they have in the solution. And just as with other endeavors, the more practice students have in thinking, the better they become at problem solving and the more they invest in the process of learning about life.

This paradigm provides a valuable template for analyzing the cause of behavior as well as providing an understanding of how to influence its change. A key factor is developing interventions that align with the perspective of the "behavee." Without this provision, interventions are often determined on the basis of how the student's behavior affects the adult, and so success is delayed or undermined.

Choices and the Attention-Getter

A first-year teacher told of a student who was giving her some difficulty in class. One particular day, true to form, the student was turning around in his seat, talking to his neighbors, and offering smart-alecky answers in response to the teacher's attempt to engage him in the lesson.

Eventually the teacher reached the limit of her tolerance for such conduct. Remembering something about giving kids choices, she said to the student, "You can do one of two things: you can stay in class and behave, or you can go to the office now."

In response, the kid left the room, made a comment that only intensified the teacher's irritation, and slammed the door. The teacher wondered why the so-often-recommended technique of giving kids options didn't work.

Although we could debate how the choices were given, the actual alternatives themselves, or even the timing, there is a more compelling issue to consider: whether this particular strategy was the most appropriate one in the first place.

It seems apparent that the student was engaged in behavior that would draw attention to himself. Given the Four Key Principles as a paradigm for analysis, it would further seem that attention-getting behavior is most consistent with self-concept issues. The way the choices were administered by the teacher would have been much more appropriate in the context of a power struggle, which clearly falls into the realm of concerns about control or autonomy. The reason she used what was essentially a strategy to address control issues, as she pointed out herself, was that she *felt like* she was involved in a power struggle with this kid.

Armed with this new perspective, the teacher investigated the kid's background. She found out that his mother had abandoned him and that he had been in four foster homes. He had been in a number of schools within the past several years. He was currently living with his grandmother, who by all appearances didn't really want him. Essentially, the teacher concluded, this kid felt he didn't belong—anywhere. One might also suspect he was attempting to increase his status among his peers. The teacher's interaction, without any intention of doing so, simply perpetuated the source of the problem.

The teacher then made a conscious decision to use self-concept strategies on the kid. She used the bonding mechanisms of smiles, eye contact, and touch. She also made liberal use of techniques that validated the kid's personhood. Within just a few weeks, the relationship between the teacher and student had strengthened significantly. Discipline was no longer a problem, and the teacher grew to legitimately like the kid.

From Zero to Attack Mode in a Nanosecond

I was called to a meeting about a seventh-grade kid whose behavior was so inappropriate that an alternative program was being considered. The adults working with this student had exhausted their energies and didn't know what else to do.

From the description given to me, I anticipated this seventh-grader would be over six feet tall, weigh at least two hundred pounds, and display constant aggression. When I got to the meeting, sitting among the myriad of adults was a mousy-looking, scrawny little kid sitting in a semifetal position. My first thought was, "Where's the kid we're meeting about?" Imagine my surprise when he was pointed out.

As questions were asked, this kid said "I don't know" to most of those directed at him, and shrugged his shoulders at the rest. This seemed so unlike what I'd heard about the kid, who reportedly mouthed off to security officers, administrators, and teachers without a moment's notice.

Within a few days, however, I had an opportunity to see, firsthand, a confrontive interaction between this student and the administrator. It was then I saw that there had been little exaggeration. This kid showed absolutely no fear, no intimidation, and no sign of backing down. There was no quiver of his lip, nor diversion of his eye contact—nothing that resembled the reclusive little kid I'd seen at that first meeting. Actually, he reminded me of a cornered animal who was more than willing to fight to the death.

A few days later, the teacher intimated to me she had grown to dislike this kid. However, as we talked, it seemed rather that she had a very strong bond with this student and a strong desire to work with him. Her dislike was really a way of coping with the feeling that she was not succeeding. By the end of that almost hour-long conversation, she had come to see the kid's behavior from a different perspective, and her interactions with him changed as a result.

As I eventually found out, this kid truly believed that no one in the whole school liked him. Because he believed nobody cared about him, he concluded there was every reason to defend himself at the slightest provocation. Once this kid's perception was understood, it was relatively easy to see that the interventions (which were essentially face-offs) that had been utilized were actually exacerbating the problem. This was very much a kid who felt he didn't belong, whose need for validation was not being met at school. Through his behavior, he was trying to get what he needed.

Replacement Behavior

A key factor in working successfully with students is helping them develop replacement behavior that will meet the same need prompting the misconduct. In the past, some educators were simply interested in stopping the offensive actions. However, a common phenomenon was that students filled the void with something even worse. Another oft-used practice was to influence behavior change by providing tangible incentives. In actuality, this process is fraught with the potential of creating satiation. Rewards that work in the beginning can lose their effectiveness in quick order.

When a student engages in a maladaptive behavior, it is for a reason. When rewards or punishments are administered that are different from what was maintaining the behavior in the first place, there may be some short-term effect (e.g., honeymoon period), but little chance of long-term change. For instance, it is somewhat perplexing why, if a student misbehaves out of a desire to be validated by the teacher's attention, anyone would think that this behavior would permanently change upon the offering of free time on the computer, a happy face on a chart, or detention after school.

Invoking the Power of the Military

Behavior changes on a long-term basis only when thinking is changed. I long ago realized that when, as a teacher, my modus operandi was to simply force a kid to change by overpowering him or her, I often became the target of a coup attempt. What I have learned, however, is that if kids are provided information in a way that changes their thinking, then adults have a lot more influence, and positive change, rather than overthrow, is the more common result.

I recall one student, Zeke, who had a history of fairly violent behavior. He once smashed the windows of his sister's car and even in middle school would often draw pictures of violent acts. He had long stated that he wanted to join the military when he graduated, an idea that made many of his teachers shudder.

By the time Zeke was halfway through high school, he had changed significantly. There was still some residual braggadocio, but he was maintaining his grades and had joined the wrestling team. He still had a temper, but it ignited only occasionally.

One day it flared up badly. Zeke had a sense of justice that was pretty defined, and a teacher had violated one of his fundamental rules. Unbeknownst to this teacher, another had given Zeke permission to explore a topic on the Internet. The first teacher acted on her presumption that Zeke should have been working on his math and threatened him with disciplinary action if he didn't comply. In Zeke's mind, she had drawn first blood.

I had known Zeke since he was in third grade, and as we talked about the incident, he said, "Tell those f- - - ing bastards about my history so they will know what I am capable of." Zeke was definitely not in a thinking state at this point, and I knew that telling him that threats and vulgar language were against school rules would only escalate the situation.

In times like this, we really have to appeal to the values of the other person. Zeke absolutely thought he was in the right, and I knew he very much wanted to be a soldier. So, instead of moralizing (or reminding him about the school's conduct code), I asked the following question: "Zeke, I know you want to go into the military when you are done with school, and I am wondering what the recruiters might think if they knew that you lose control when under pressure."

I still remember the change that came over this young man. He didn't say anything, but the glare in his eyes changed within seconds. I really do think, after a couple more years of practice in thinking, Zeke will make a wonderful soldier and do his nation proud.

The Winning Combination

I CLOSE THIS CHAPTER with an excerpt from a paper submitted by a special education administrator who attended one of my graduate classes. Note how she blended special education procedure and Love and Logic to obtain a positive outcome for a situation that could have been more than disastrous:

> I decided I would use Love and Logic in a meeting where a parent, staff, and a student were gathered for the purpose of a review of a behavioral incident and the consequences that needed to be developed. The scenario I used was the outcome of a student's sexually explicit advances to both male and female peers. The young boy was arrested and suspended from school. After being released, and prior to a pending removal from the home, the young boy was going to be returned to school for two weeks. The meeting was set up to define the parameters of his return. There were thirteen people in the conference room, including an angry parent, an advocate, the student, four caseworkers, teachers, principals, a social worker, a guidance counselor, and myself [the district administrator].
>
> The meeting started with the parent demanding that any unfair treatment of the boy's reinstatement would not be tolerated. Based on Love and Logic, I used an empathetic

response, clearly defined my intentions, and thanked the parent for caring enough about his son to express his concern. That worked well to defuse the parent's initial hostility. As the meeting continued, the parent and the advocate demanded that the boy be in the physical education class. I stated that all students had the right to be safe from unwanted touching and asked the parent, the student, and all others if they could agree to that. They all agreed and then I stepped out on the limb of "shared control" and asked the parent if he would allow the boy to determine what needed to be done with the physical education problem. Amazingly, he agreed. Having read Love and Logic, I knew I'd have to be open to options other than the ones I'd thought of, but needed to be ready to accept the consequences the boy came up with. I used a calm voice, expressed empathy for his poor choices, and then let it ride.

He ultimately decided to walk in the halls with an aide for thirty minutes or sit in the social worker's office and play card games for the class period. Most staff would rather have had him leave school for the day, but they all agreed to the solution.

Buoyed by success, we continued along until the topic of lunchtime came up. The boy, the vice principal, and the parent got into a rather heated discussion about where and when he would eat. I stopped the argument by using an adapted one-liner from "Funk and Fay's Famous Phrases." I said, "I've got an idea that I think no one will like!" I suggested a preposterous idea about not having lunch and lopping the time off at the end of the day. It stopped the argument, but did garner some angry and surprised looks. I expressed my feelings about the argument, stated the problem, and asked if we could agree to let the boy come up with a solution. Again, it worked quite well.

The two-hour meeting had its ups and downs, but in the end a schedule for the young man had been determined. The parameters for his daily comings and goings were accepted by all the participants and the parent left without a cloud of hostility floating above him.

The boy, I felt, left with a sense of ownership on how his day was going to be structured and what the expectations for him were. I left chuckling to myself and shaking my head because I couldn't believe it worked as well as it had. In reflecting, I felt the way Dave Funk does when he noted in his book *Love and Logic Solutions for Kids with Special Needs* that although there are circumstances which would exclude the use of Love and Logic, for a large number of situations, Love and Logic can be applied and create a win/win outcome.

I like being able to set up a reciprocal relationship in meetings because the level of honesty and trust goes up. Love and Logic helped me to stay calm and not assume ownership for the problem. It is hard, though, when those around you want to hand the problem to you on a silver platter. Using the principles of Love and Logic also helped to keep the meeting focused on a common goal and not waste energy fighting one another. Establishing a trusting and thinking relationship kept the problem the problem, rather than allowing it to become a catalyst for useless arguments.

Although this is but one story about how Love and Logic works in the trenches, it is representative of innumerable experiences from parents, educators, and others who work with kids.

Chapter 2

The Behavior Connection

The primary motive of human volitional behavior
is to enhance a sense of self-worth
and to avoid a sense of failure.

— ARTHUR COMBS

Behavior Is Global

IN THE FIELD OF EDUCATION, behavior is global. Whether the focus is on emotional stability, academic skill development, or social appropriateness, behavior permeates the purpose of going to school.

A common presumption is that groups of duly qualified professionals can analyze behavior problems and develop effective interventions. Information obtained from such analysis, the reasoning goes, determines the cause for the problem and what corrective action needs to be taken.

But analysis is not exempt from presuppositions. In this chapter, we will examine a basis for understanding volitional behavior within the context of Love and Logic principles. Essentially, the question to be addressed is: Why do people do what they do, even when it doesn't seem to be in their long-term best interest? To be effective with kids, we need to know not only what to do when things go bad, but also how to maintain a learning environment that reduces the reasons kids misbehave in the first place.

The Payoff for Misbehavior Is Evidently Worth the Price

A primary consideration is that misbehavior is a maladaptive way to get a legitimate need met. A substantial part of justifying this statement is the universal human characteristic that everyone can vindicate their own behavior.

Another factor is that whatever a person anticipates getting or avoiding from their behavior is evidently worth the effort and risk. Once this "function" is determined, we have the key to knowing what will likely maintain any replacement behavior that is considered less detrimental.

As commonsense as this may seem, too often adults develop behavior interventions that provide a consequence or reinforcement that is unrelated to what was maintaining the maladaptive behavior. Sometimes those who develop the plans choose what is administratively convenient, theoretically plausible, or based on the adult's preferences. Even worse, sometimes the payoff is simply an item on a predetermined list (e.g., free time, stickers, detentions) of rewards and punishments that have become traditional within the institution.

I recall a student who had been given ninety-two Saturday detentions by April of his junior year. When the administrator was questioned about the wisdom of this penalty (and regardless, how could all the detentions be served within the time the student still had left in school?), he simply stated it was the only action he thought was available to him. There was evidently little consideration of how many of these detentions would have to be given before the realization set in that this strategy was not working.

Although such interventions may have some short-term success, we may actually have a situation analogous to vinegar-and-oil salad dressing. That is, as long as the mixture is shaken vigorously, everything kind of blends together and we get what is wanted for the moment. However, stop the artificial outside forces and the two components show their true characteristics and separate completely. When strategies are developed that don't really address the source of the problem on a long-term basis, more likely than not the maladaptive behavior resumes, and sometimes with a vengeance.

Determining a Presuppositional Base

Since presuppositions to a large degree determine outcomes (especially in the arena of human behavior), establishing operational definitions is vital. Relevant factors need to be incorporated into the development of a paradigm that will offer a practical format within a sound theoretical base. Love and Logic is based on the understanding that the brain develops patterns that have two primary functions: (1) making sense of the world, and (2) protecting selfhood.

Information that is contrary to the established pattern is often discounted, reinterpreted, or perhaps not even perceived. One only has to watch a group of old men on any particular morning at any given restaurant talking about any conceivable topic (but especially politics or sports) to see this fully demonstrated.

This brain process of forming patterns results in the development of a perceptual base. The important factor when dealing with behavior is that humans act consistent with their perceptions. The complicating factor is that there are as many nuances of perception as there are persons involved with any given situation. Understanding how a kid perceives a specific situation takes skill and understanding, and a willingness on the part of the professional to see the situation through the eyes of another.

A second function of the brain is to protect what makes us a person. This function is located deep within the primal portions of the brain and is pretty much automatic. All sensory information goes through the emotional centers of the brain first, much of which is insufficient to trigger any emotional response at all. However, everyone has had the experience of going into "brain stem" mode and feeling the very basics of human emotion.

The Wake-Up Call

Many years ago I was asked to speak in a small town in Michigan. After finishing my teaching of a graduate class, I started out from southern Wisconsin on a Sunday night. As I reached the northern suburbs of Chicago, I became quite sleepy and decided to park in a lot that seemed available. I parked in a driveway just off the road, faced my car toward the highway (in case I wasn't supposed to be there and had to make my exit with as little awkwardness as possible), and promptly went to sleep.

How long I slept, I don't know, but I do remember the waking-up part. I looked out through my windshield and saw cars whizzing by me at breakneck speed. My first fuzzy thought was that I had fallen asleep at the wheel and was now about to be involved in a multicar pileup. Consistent with that perception, I slammed on the brakes as hard as I could. But instead of coming to a crashing halt, I quickly realized I was parked and already stopped. Slamming on the brakes of a car that is not moving and whose engine is off is really quite unproductive. The point to be made is that my behavior was consistent with my perception.

The Puzzlement

What becomes crucial, however, is how the purpose of behavior is to be defined and just how many "functions" govern human volitional behavior. This becomes psychological, if not actually philosophical, because of the overwhelming influence of the perceptual set of the person doing the evaluating.

For instance, if the evaluator holds to a mechanistic view of behavior, determinations will probably be made in the language of operant conditioning, with recommendations that reflect stimulus-response remedies. On the other hand, if the evaluator has a more cognitive behavioral view, the interaction of the student and environment will be emphasized. If the evaluator has essentially a spiritual view of human behavior, the conclusions will be skewed to this orientation, with interventions based on moral decision-making with assistance from the divine.

What I would emphasize is that we all have, and indeed need, some pattern by which information is made purposeful. What that pattern consists of is important, because it will influence decisions and conclusions. However, regardless of what orientation the evaluator has, a person's behavior results in (1) avoiding something that is disliked, or (2) obtaining something that is wanted. A third category has also been identified—behavior that is self-stimulatory—but upon observation, even this type of behavior can be subsumed under the previous two.

I have always been interested in searching for universals of human behavior—those factors that circumvent culture and are basically true for all people all of the time. I also recognize that this may be an impossible task; however, when we observe a wide variety of people in a number of diverse situations, we can at least get some operational concepts that can be generally applied to most people most of the time.

Humans engage in volitional behavior for relatively few basic reasons. Furthermore, behavior that becomes the focus of concern is usually not considered maladaptive by the student, at least when engaging in the behavior. Therefore the perspective of the student must be considered if an accurate analysis is to be accomplished and effective interventions are to be developed.

Whatever structure is used, the real question is: What aspects of psychological being are people desperate to protect? Love and Logic encapsulates an answer within its Four Key Principles:

1. *Self-concept:* Perhaps the deepest part of ourselves can be termed "personhood." We actively seek to enhance our sense of self-worth and avoid a sense of failure. Self-concept is the survival factor that forms the perception we have of ourselves. Self-concept, in turn, is a building block for behavior. Those with a healthy sense of self-worth tend to have fewer discipline problems and achieve more.

   But there is a paradox: There appears to be little "self" in self-concept. Additionally, what we think other people think about us comes from the implied, or covert, messages we receive, far more than it comes from what is actually said overtly. Educators need to know this when interacting with students and realize that nonverbal aspects of interaction will affect the students to a far greater extent than just the words spoken.

   When there is a perception of attack on self-concept, defense mechanisms are engaged. Many students involved in significant discipline issues often adopt the stance coined by James Rafini: "If I can't win, at least I can avoid losing." In a society such as ours, where worth and ability are equated, students will engage in sometimes extreme behavior to divert attention away from weaknesses that imply lack of innate ability.

   Correlated with self-concept is a sense of belonging. We tend to be social creatures in need of social acceptance. In situations where this sense of belonging is either lacking or violated, there is a tendency to do whatever is necessary to satisfy this need, even if it means joining a group not known for its wholesomeness.

2. *Shared control:* The need for control or power appears to be an innate human characteristic. In a sense, personhood is validated by influencing the environment. However, autonomy issues also become classic sources of power struggles. We want freedom to determine our outcomes, and when we cannot exert control that satisfies this need, we are willing to substitute control over other people or situations.

One paradox often not recognized by teachers is that the more power they take away from students with control issues, the more covert and sophisticated the unwanted behaviors become. Many teachers have the feeling that to control students, all of the power must be taken from them so they cannot fight back. The end result, however, is that the scene is set for a power struggle the student will, in all probability, win. Students will often do an "end run" and will create "new and improved" ways of sabotaging the adult.

In one extreme case, a student accused a teacher of inappropriate touching. The student's story was false, but she did "get back" at the teacher in a way that eventually destroyed his career. Usually, a student's plan to undermine a teacher is not so dramatic, but the everyday chipping away at a teacher's authority (and eventual sanity) causes teaching to lose its fun and does not promote effective behavior management. Whether overt or passive, control factors are a primary consideration as a function of behavior.

3. *Empathy with consequence:* How many times have we disregarded something because it "made no sense"? A classic example is students serving detention when such penalty has no logical relationship to the infraction. A primary function of the brain is to develop patterns to make sense of the world. When students perceive that there is little logical connection between what they do and what happens to them, their reactions, although perfectly logical from their own perspective, may well appear problematic to an observer. In addition, when external forces inflict "contrived consequences" that seem unfair, and seem to have no connection with the issue at hand, the element of predictability diminishes. Since predictability is an essential component of trust and security, "artificial consequences" serve to maintain the very behavior they are intended to extinguish.

Because consequences are such an individualized aspect of human existence, it is vitally important to ensure that the student's perception be a prime consideration. What may be considered a punishment by the evaluator may actually be considered a reward by the student.

Take, for example, the student who gains increased status with his peers because he "takes" everything the principal can dish out without flinching. Even if the eventual outcome will be to develop a behavior management plan, to know how the student sees the conduct should be an essential part of the process.

A balance of empathy with consequences is a magic combination. Whereas it may be more "natural" to substitute empathy with prophecy ("Do this again and something worse will happen."), pity ("You poor, poor, dear."), or reminder ("Didn't I tell you this would get you into trouble?"), to do so really gives the "consequensee" an opportunity to avoid responsibility by denying and arguing. However, when a student's plight is given an empathetic response, the pain of unwise decisions most often remains until dealt with.

4. *Shared thinking:* Almost always, it will benefit a team of educators to understand the offending behavior from the student's perspective. This is not to condone or approve—simply to see the problem the way the kid does. Since the best source of the student's perspective is the student, having everyone in the thinking, rather than emotional, state would seem the preferred position. When stress is reduced and kids are free to think, the likelihood of getting accurate information from them is significantly increased.

    To be sure, we all think within the parameters of our perception. If someone considers their behavior justifiable, little will change until their thinking does. If attempts are made to change thinking by confrontation or even evidence alone, the chances of success are limited. Rather, there has to be some point that is accepted as unarguable by any of the individuals involved. That is, all parties need to get to a point of mutual agreement before any significant progress can be made. This is where philosophy has a practical application.

Remember Descartes? He originated the phrase "I think, therefore I am" as a way of establishing a foundation for proving that "self" exists. Even though almost everything else can be denied, if I can contemplate anything, I must exist to do so. This is a clue for how to change people's thinking. If we start at the point that agreement (i.e., an undeniable point of common understanding) is obtained, a foundation for change is established.

As a simple example, imagine a student disrupting a class and being confronted by the teacher with, "Why do you think you can come into my class all of the time, acting like some idiot and constantly messing things up?" Imagine the opportunity that "all of the time," "idiot," "constantly," and "messing up" give the kid to entrench. More often than not, these words encourage the kid to intensify the very behavior the adult wants to change. Addressing the conduct is the ultimate goal, but if the kid's thinking doesn't change, good luck with the behavior!

Compare another way to initiate the conversation: "It seems that you and I have a different view of how this class should be run—would you agree?" This is a classic "one-sentence intervention" and there is a significantly high chance the kid will say "yes" (in one form or another). Then, at least the beginnings of a foundation are set and the conversation has a much better chance of being linear. For instance, the next comment by the adult might be, "Would you be willing to work with me to make some changes?"— a phrase that would be dangerous, if not impossible, in the previous scenario.

Hurt Back or Hide a Weakness

If it is true that perception is the driving force of behavior, a significant part of developing interventions would be to determine how students perceive the purpose of their own actions. As simplistic as it may sound, it seems that maladaptive volitional behavior is engaged in either to hide a weakness or to inflict on another the hurt one feels. In my experience of working with kids with conduct problems, there appear to be few exceptions.

One student who had been referred to me was not completing assignments, and even those he worked on were often not handed in. As a result, his grades were being significantly affected. The behavior of concern was eventually defined as "not finishing work and not handing work in." Not the most sophisticated of wording, perhaps, but wording that everyone understood.

The next step was to identify the function of the behavior. In this case, the student readily identified the "payoff." He said he didn't understand many of the assignments and would be embarrassed to hand them in poorly done or ask questions in class and thus look "dumb" in front of his peers. Once the student was consulted, the reason for his behavior was simple to identify: to keep himself from being embarrassed (a self-preservation issue, which upon final analysis is much healthier than a self-destruction issue).

The next step was to identify a replacement behavior that would address the target behavior (in this case, completing and handing in work) and get the same (affective) payoff. The student didn't want to feel embarrassed (which in fact is a healthy motivation) and was in the best position to identify a replacement behavior that would not cause him to feel awkward in front of his peers.

His answer was very simple. He would initiate questions with his special education teacher within the context of a resource room and talk privately to his regular education teachers. Of necessity, everyone needed to know this plan, so it would not be unintentionally sabotaged (for example, to avoid having a teacher publicly asking the student if he needed help during regular class time). What this also meant was that the student would be allowed, without interference, to engage in behavior that was formerly considered unproductive (sitting and doing nothing). What to some might have appeared to be a short-term problem was in actuality a long-term solution.

I'd Rather Be Bad Than Dumb

Calib was a fourth-grader described as oppositional-defiant and basically uncontrollable. Once when he was removed from class, he did not reach the office as anticipated. While all of the adults were out searching, he made his way to the PA system and announced, "I'm in the office now, you a--holes." Shortly thereafter, the staff decided to shell out some money and buy some time from a behavior specialist.

As the expert observed, she'd noticed Calib committing an unsolicited act of kindness for a kindergarten girl who was coming down the stairs with her shoes untied. With true compassion in his voice, Calib cautioned her that loose laces could be dangerous and then tied them for her.

In the process of developing a behavior plan, the specialist recommended that Calib work with students in a second-grade classroom. Although the teachers had some trepidation, they implemented a plan. The second-grade teacher had a large class and could especially use help when her students had to change location (e.g., from the classroom to recess). Calib not only did an exemplary job, but also showed a level of care for the safety and welfare of the younger students that no one at the school had seen before. In addition, his behavior in his own classroom improved.

Upon analysis, the function of Calib's behavior was a self-concept issue. His academic skills were deficient and he did not want to be viewed as having lack of ability. As with most kids, he would rather be considered just about anything than dumb. When he was able to use his interpersonal and verbal skills in an altruistic situation, he could demonstrate his strengths, and these became a foundation for behavior change. Whereas his teachers initially attributed his behavior to negative factors, eventually they recognized that he was simply fulfilling a basic need (e.g., to enhance his sense of self-worth)—but in a way that caused problems for others.

Affective Aspects of Behavior Interventions

In the development of behavior interventions, the chances of success rely on a number of factors. Much has been written about the necessary components of these plans, including reinforcement contingencies, environmental changes, and other considerations typically associated with behavior management. However, regardless of what else is involved, the affective aspects of behavior should not be overlooked.

Although two obvious issues concern self-worth and autonomy, a starting point is a student's sense of "ownership" for any plan that might be developed. If the student perceives a behavior plan as just another way that adults are trying to manipulate him or her, there will logically be resistance.

In developing formal plans to change a student's behavior, the adults will often devise a punishment or reward that is in an entirely different domain than what is motivating the student in the first place. For instance, a student may be engaging in a misbehavior for reasons of gaining self-validation (e.g., disrupting to gain attention). If the consequences for the replacement behavior (i.e., not disrupting) are based on what is effective for control issues (e.g., giving choices), there may be some noticeable change in the student's behavior simply because of the incidental adult interaction. However, any positive effect is short-term at best, and the plan is easily sabotaged.

Rather than dwelling on consequences that are administratively convenient and available to the teacher, or on consequences that adult members of the team might think to be personally reinforcing, it would seem that what is already maintaining a student's undesirable behavior should be utilized. After all, whatever the perceived payoff consists of, it is maintaining an inappropriate behavior against worthy odds, as in the following example:

Much time and effort had been expended by staff to find a replacement behavior to curb a young student's verbally aggressive behavior. At one point the student informed her teachers that cursing was really what made her feel better, and that counting backward from ten (the replacement behavior the adults preferred) did not. The student had actually indicated what a reinforcer could be (i.e., cursing); however, this was part and parcel of what often got her into trouble. A suggestion was made that she be taught to exercise what had already been demonstrated as being reinforcing/cathartic, but in a way that would not get her into more trouble. For instance, there are two ways to curse—out loud or silently. To curse silently (a behavior that most of us exercise) would be closer to "normal" and fairly adaptive, and would have the added benefit of not getting the student into trouble. An additional benefit was that it seemed a far easier job for the teachers to accomplish than to continue their limited success with trying to teach this student a behavior that was more of an irritation to her than an effective strategy.

Making Sure It's a Right Fit

Identifying interventions and prescribing medication carry similar risks. Imagine telling a physician you have severe headaches and being given some salve for warts. Imagine the emotional irritation, in addition to the continued pain, if you found out the physician prescribed wart salve for everything because it worked for some people (i.e., those with warts).

However, too often in education, this is just what happens. Teachers will say a kid is not doing their homework, or that another kid is disrupting the class, and they want to know what to do. Many times, they are really asking: What is a fairly effortless strategy that will take care of any problem the kid may have in the classroom and, by the way, take care of the problem immediately without need for change on the adult's part? Too often, substantially more thought has gone into what to do to kids when they misbehave than into preventing the misbehavior in the first place.

That, alone, would be bad enough, but what is worse is that, without an adequate understanding of how behavior is influenced, interventions may actually contribute to maintaining the problem behavior. I recall one situation in which an especially recalcitrant student had wedged himself under a low-lying table and was refusing to come out. The principal was on the floor talking with him.

Picture this not-petite woman with a too short skirt, on her knees, face to the floor, with her rear end raised immodestly. She was trying to cajole the student out by making such statements as, ". . . of course you have friends, lots of people like you." First of all, this was not true. Hardly anyone could tolerate this kid. Second, he had serious control problems, and what could be more satisfying to a kid like this than to get the principal in a very compromised position and tell him lies?

No doubt the principal was sincere. She was trying her best to make this kid feel good. And that is just the problem—she was trying, not succeeding. Not only was her interaction ineffective, but it was also, at a minimum, maintaining the very behavior she was trying to reduce.

Intervention Principles

It would be relatively easy to list a bunch of strategies with the admonition to go forth and conquer. I have learned from painful experience not to do this, especially in a book where there is little opportunity for interactive feedback. There is a tendency in education to want strategies that have an almost mathematical precision. However, behavior management is conditioned by situational variables and will require modifications to fit the kid, the circumstance, or both. Failure to individualize is usually the death knell for even the best of strategies.

So instead of listing a number of specific interventions, it seems better to look at some overall principles that, if observed and implemented, significantly increase the chances of success:

Consider the needs of all those involved. Some time ago I attended a meeting to discuss a student's behavior. He was one of the most skilled experts in passive-resistive behavior I'd ever seen. He was in tenth grade and his records showed he'd had at least five years of practice in this behavior. From the ensuing discussion, it was apparent that the adults had put much more effort into this kid's behavior than he had. It was the adults, not the kid, who were frustrated and resentful as a result. The adults felt they were being taken advantage of, and in fact they were—and building tremendous animosity toward the kid as well. Interventions are seldom effective if the adults feel they are being sucked dry. At least a partial answer to this is to ensure the kid is more invested in the problem than are the adults. This brings us to our next point.

Ensure the kid is invested. I fully realize others may disagree, but I believe that the vast majority of students (even those considered disabled) should have some involvement in the development of their own behavior interventions. After all, it is *their* behavior, and if they have no investment, there is little incentive for them to take responsibility for change. I recall many meetings populated with only the adults involved, because some thought the topic of behavior was too sensitive for a student to hear.

I fully accept that a student's involvement must be appropriate to their development and capacity. However, what I have experienced is that, in most cases, the kids pretty much know there is something the matter with them. I have also observed that, if they don't have accurate information, kids often conclude that their lot in life is worse than it really is. Kids who have trouble reading will conclude that they are dumb, and those with emotional problems will believe that they are crazy. Such inaccurate decisions only make the problem worse.

I have also been in situations where the kid was purposely excluded from attending meetings because the adults feared he or she would reveal some awkward circumstance about the home or classroom. Other times it actually seemed that the adults *wanted* the child to be dysfunctional, to fulfill some warped sense of purpose. When the student is not involved, the whole process of behavior management becomes much more burdensome. Many teams agonize over what to do with a kid when it is the kid who could give a ready answer.

I recall working with a student who had a serious behavior disorder. He thought he was all right (as should have been expected) and wanted to be in all-regular classes. Our relationship was strong enough for me to ask him if he knew why he was in special education. His predicable response focused on the faults of others.

The reports in his file listed him as having a particular condition (Asperger's syndrome), and I asked him if he knew what this meant. He didn't, and I offered to provide him with some information, with a challenge to prove the diagnosis wrong and thus that he did not need special education intervention.

A week later we met again. He was not so belligerent this time, and asked a very penetrating question: "Why didn't anyone tell me this before." It emphasized to me that avoiding talking with kids about realities is not a way to build resiliency.

Enlist enforceable conditions. Love and Logic talks much about the importance of enforceable statements. When developing effective behavior interventions, this same principle applies. There are few easier ways to sabotage a behavior plan than to put a condition that the adult cannot follow through on.

A college-aged daughter of a friend of mine had made some not wise decisions regarding the person she was having a relationship with. As a result, she had accumulated significant debt because of her boyfriend's spending. The parents counseled her about the decisions she was making and gave her sound advice. However, this advice was not heeded (a common occurrence with those in the process of learning wisdom). The parents stated that they would no longer pay their daughter's credit card and telephone bills. They had complete control over this financial aspect and could enforce it. Conditions that can't be enforced are hardly worth contemplating.

Satisfy the need driving the maladaptive behavior. So often, a behavior plan is developed seemingly irrespective of the individual student. Jim, a sophomore with Asperger's syndrome, was a budding lawyer. One of the characteristics of this disability is that those who suffer from it tenaciously hold on to concepts. In Jim's case, it was the concept of an inordinate sense of fair play. Problems were constantly arising because of his skill at pointing out the inconsistencies committed by the adults. One day, for instance, the vice principal confiscated his police scanner, with the reasoning that such devices were banned according to the student handbook.

Jim, of course, consulted the student handbook and pointed out that the ban was on two-way radios during the school day. His argument was that a police scanner was a one-way receiver and that he only used his on the bus. Technically, he was right, but he made his points in a not kind and gentle way. After making his statement, he slid the handbook, with a sarcastic flare and opened to the appropriate page, across the table, stating that if the administrator had any brains at all, she would get off her "fat a--" and quit violating her own rules. Jim also got into lots of classroom trouble, because he thought the teacher, by not giving him a chance to defend his position, was not giving him equitable treatment.

His sense of fairness or justice may have been distorted, elemental, and annoying; however, it was consistent. The intervention was basically an agreement that within twenty-four hours (with the exception of weekends and breaks) he would be given a formal opportunity to plead his case. That was the only intervention needed.

Concentrate on internalizing the control. One thing I know for sure is that we eventually satiate on tangible reinforcers. Also, for some kids, the tangible reinforcer they would work for is way out of reach of the average school budget. In addition, whatever is maintaining a maladaptive behavior is almost always (I can't think of an exception) internalized. If this is so, why do we think external reinforcers will do the trick? Even a kleptomaniac is stealing to satisfy some internalized urge. Any assessment used to address a behavior problem should certainly determine what is driving the behavior.

Change the student's perception about the offending behavior.
Altering kids' perception about what they are doing is a very big step
toward some permanent changes. Rather than dwelling on whether or
not a behavior is wrong, asking if the behavior is working out well may
result in a much more productive conversation. Most kids can accept
that behaviors that get them into trouble are misplaced rather than bad
or evil. And the honest fact is, often the behaviors that are a problem
in the classroom would not be in another environment.

Do adults get into trouble at a conference for visiting with a friend?
How many people get into trouble for swearing when their favorite
sports team loses a game because of avoidable errors? Do adults get into
trouble for chewing gum? Does it make sense, then, that kids are mostly
sharp enough to figure out that many behaviors are not innately bad?

So, to a degree, having the student learn where "offending" conduct
is acceptable and where it is not, is part of the process of changing
behavior. I remember working with one student who used off-color
words quite often. Since this behavior didn't seem to be maintained by
the reaction of others, the intervention was simply having the student
make two lists. One list concerned where "those words" could be said
and not be a problem. The other list concerned where those words
would cause trouble. The kid adhered to the conditions he came up
with, and that was the end of it.

If these basic principles are not observed, there is tremendous risk that
interventions that will actually make the problem worse may be implemented.

The Three-Inch Solution

As educators, unfortunately, there seems to be a constant need to
remind ourselves to keep the kid in the picture. A number of years ago
a student was demonstrating some quite disconcerting behavior.

Several times per week he would rise from his seat, shout some novel curse or vulgarity, and throw some selected item to the floor. Whereupon the teacher would send the kid to the office for some "disciplining." More often than not, the principal was busy and the student, biding his time upon a chair in the outer office, promptly started to read (he always took a book with him upon removal from the classroom).

The adults met numerous times to discuss this student and devise a plan to reduce this behavior. Nothing worked for more than a very few days. Finally, discouraged and bedraggled, they asked for an outside expert to help.

This "expert" asked for the kid to be present at a meeting to discuss what to do. At that meeting, one of the first questions was addressed to the kid, asking him if he knew why he was there. The kid answered, "Because I say bad words, break things, and slam the door." Then, evidently for the first time, the kid was asked, "Do you know why you do these things?" To which the kid said, "Yes, because I don't like sitting close to people and sometimes I just want to get away for a while."

That was good information, and the "expert" then asked the student why he didn't simply make a polite request to move himself to a more comfortable place. The student's response provided the key: "If I ask nicely to go someplace to be alone, the teacher tells me to sit down and shut up. Doing what I do is the only way I can get away."

Armed with this information and knowing that the teacher had the room configured so groups of four student desks were butted up against each other in little colonies, the kid was asked how far away his desk would have to be in order for him not to feel like he had to get away. "Three inches," was the kid's reply.

That was the intervention! Now, the kid did measure the distance several times a day (still a left-of-center behavior to be sure), but this replacement behavior met the same need as what was reinforcing the maladaptive behavior and, as such, was equally maintained.

Preparing for the Inevitable

A CONSISTENT COMMENT I HEAR when presenting Love and Logic goes something like this: "Yeah, I can see how this works when you are alone with a kid, but I have a gaggle of kids in my classroom and half of them are special ed—what do I do? I can't just leave my classroom and have a nice private talk with a kid who is misbehaving." What requires professional-level thinking is how to work within the given variables. I may not be able to talk with a kid during class, and may have to call them at home during the evening. As my departed Grandma often reminded me, "Where there is a will, there is a way."

Frankly, lots of strategies that work with kids on a one-to-one basis can be adapted quite easily to groups. However, an aspect more critical than specific strategies is to reduce the factors that can sabotage our best efforts. Principals can nix a plan they don't agree with. Other teachers and parents can undermine opportunities to be successful with kids.

Although perhaps regrettable, people come to the table with preconceived notions, some of which we have little control over. I recall one such instance when a parent was hypercritical of a new teacher and oft-commented that she was "so young." However, the year this teacher got married, this same parent congratulated her and the relationship turned positive. Nothing else much changed, but the teacher was evidently now worthy of having this parent's respect.

First impressions last for a long time, and getting started right is vitally important, but even more so is maintaining the course. First impressions are just that—first, and a one-shot deal at that. So the wise teacher does whatever possible to set the stage for success.

Gather the Troops

There is a strategy we have all known since childhood. I used it often when I did something that my siblings could "tell on me" about. I came to learn early on that whoever got to my parents first usually had the most influence. Whether it be labeled "proactive," or just "getting a leg up," this strategy is still a viable principle.

When planning a new year, and especially if changes in teaching style or strategy are in mind, this "being first to tell" strategy can be of great benefit. When preparing for any school year, there are only a few people who are intimately involved in what we do: principals, parents, teachers, secretaries, and custodians. It is best that these people know what we are doing right from the start, so they don't inadvertently (or even directly) sabotage worthy efforts to help kids.

Field Trips and Tour Guides

Some years ago a teacher told me that her first "field trip" of the year is a tour, led by the custodians and secretaries, of the "intimate" parts of the building. Her kids get to see how the phone system works and the room where all the copies are made. They get to explore the boiler room and see "behind the scenes" plumbing. Boys and girls get to see each other's restrooms (and so eliminate a lot of mystery thus associated). Kids even get to see the faculty room!

And what does this teacher get for her efforts? Besides having the cleanest room, where all the lights work, and getting favors from office staff when she needs them, she has access to ready-made colleagues to help her with the discipline of her special education kids. All she has to say is, "Would you talk to . . ."—and the wisdom and experience of those key people are at her disposal.

Keeping Coworkers from Being the Problem

A special education teacher attending one of my graduate courses told me that although she very much adhered to the Love and Logic philosophy, her principal and some teachers did not. Although she did not anticipate that these people would purposely undercut her effectiveness with kids, she also knew that they could make things rough for her if she did not tow the line.

Her strategy was always to discuss with others what she intended as the end goal for any changes she made. For instance, she might say, "I want Jimmy to improve his reading," "I want to work with Susan to not be so aggressive," or "I think I know a way to get Dan's parents to help him more with his homework." Then she would establish a timeline for each of these "projects."

She would ask her coworkers to observe her working with kids and critique her performance. She even asked the principal if these "projects" could be incorporated into her yearly performance evaluation. She offered to provide periodic updates and asked her colleagues to advise her if progress seemed slower than anticipated. Since her colleagues were part of the process, there was little concern about sabotage and criticism. They were inextricably invested in having this teacher succeed.

Getting Parents on Our Side

Early in Jim Fay's stint as a principal, he thought it reasonable for kids to learn responsibility by experiencing the consequences of their own decisions. One way to do this, he reasoned, was to not bail kids out when they forgot their lunch money. Since it often seems that no good deed goes unpunished, as soon as this announcement was made, several parents began demanding his head on a platter. These parents didn't even see "responsibility" as the intent. Rather, they took Jim's action as evidence he did not love their kids.

As a result of this experience, Jim learned the value of "telling first" and wrote the following letter:

Dear Parents,

In the past, we have done a poor job of teaching your children responsibility. We have been lending them money for lunches if they forget their lunch money or sack lunch. Needless to say, we have a number of chronic forgetters. From now on, we are going to do a better job of teaching responsibility and not lend lunch money. If you feel your child is one of those few who may not be able to cope with learning the realities of life in this new way, please give me a ring and we'll talk it over personally.

There was not one call from parents.

A Test for the Teacher

Good classrooms and good teachers go together. In previous books (*Teaching with Love and Logic* and *Love and Logic Solutions for Kids with Special Needs*), the concept of consultant teaching was discussed. Reduced to the essentials, this teaching style indicates the teacher has a presence that is a balance of confidence and humility.

It is my sense that we pretty much already know the characteristics of a good teacher. I also think we can figure out what needs to be done. In some of the graduate courses I teach, I often have participants take the following very brief, yes/no "test":

1. If you were accused in a court of law of being a good teacher, would there be enough evidence to convict you?

2. If renewal of your contract were dependent upon your learning a set of new skills, do you know what characteristics you would like the instructor to have?

3. Do you exemplify the characteristics identified in the previous question?

If we sufficiently look into ourselves, we pretty much know what kids need.

And Before Any Further Ado: A Word About Extremes

Special needs students pose a wide continuum of problems in the regular classroom. At the extreme end are students who pose safety issues for themselves, other kids, and even teachers. Although the right of special needs students to be educated with nondisabled peers is acknowledged, there are some kids who I am convinced are not ready to be in a regular classroom at all. They need preparation, and that is part of their special education.

Kids with extreme needs do not need the "drip" approach to interventions. I have known some kids who need a full-immersion speech therapy program; others need a semester of nothing but anger management. Strategies for any special education kid (but especially for those with extreme needs) should not be limited by schedules, the way things have always been done, or placing kids in situations (e.g., normal educational settings) when to do so will prevent them from learning the skills they need to function in their adult world. When programming and placement of these kids are based on a distortion of "least restrictive environment," we too often try to repair the symptoms rather than treat the source. I fear that, when school is over for many of these kids, they are no better off than when they started.

Perhaps by Design: A Near Universal Principle

WHEN IT COMES TO BEHAVIOR PRINCIPLES, one I especially adhere to is that if a strategy won't work on your spouse, it probably won't work long-term on kids. Imagine giving your significant other a Saturday detention for some mistake like forgetting to finish a chore. However, a principle that does approach the universal is this: Whatever we use on kids, they will use on us.

I end this chapter with a story from a close professional colleague and friend:

Since our oldest son, Tiernan, began kindergarten this year, he has put our family on a variety of behavior management plans. The latest went like this:

Tiernan came home from school, found his notepad and pencil and matter-of-factly asked, "Mom, how do you spell 'behavior'?" I told him and then asked why he needed to know. He explained that beginning right then and there, he was going to keep track of Brennan's behavior (his three-year-old brother) and he promptly wrote "good behavior" on one page and "bad behavior" on another.

Next he asked, "Mom, how was Brennan at Joan's [the sitter] today?" I told him "Good," so Tiernan wrote down, on the "good behavior" page, "Brennan beed good at Jons."

Later, with his arm around his little brother, Tiernan explained the plan. When Brennan filled up the "good" page, upon the next trip to the store, he would get a toy—even if Mom didn't want to buy one. Tiernan also went on to explain that it didn't matter if there were things on the "bad" page (those things happen). Filling up the "good" page was all that mattered.

Shortly thereafter, Brennan, the world's best imitator, got out his own notepad and pencil, sat down at the table, and asked, "Mom, how you wite ['write'—Brennan had a bit of immature speech yet] ABC?" Keeping a straight face, I asked what he was working on. He explained, "Mom, I keep twack of yoo behavoos."

Definitely the children of a special education teacher!

The honest fact is that kids behave consistent with their instruction. The problem is that what they learn is not always what the adults intended to teach. It certainly behooves us to periodically take a look at how we are affecting children and be willing to make the necessary adjustments.

Chapter 3

Deciphering
Special Education

Disability is a natural part of the human experience and in no way diminishes the right of individuals to participate in or contribute to society. Improving educational results for children with disabilities is an essential element of our national policy of ensuring equality of opportunity, full participation, independent living, and economic self-sufficiency for individuals with disabilities.

— INDIVIDUALS WITH DISABILITIES ACT (2004)

From Then to Now

IMAGINE A TIME WHEN A STUDENT WHO DROOLED would not be allowed in school because classmates might be offended. Contemplate a world where if a student were not strong enough to carry firewood, he would be considered unfit to receive an education. Such practices had legal support in the courts and were fairly common until injured soldiers returning from Vietnam changed the perception of disability. Although the Rehabilitation Act of 1973 was developed to prevent discrimination in employing these veterans, it eventually resulted in a

49

profoundly new understanding of disability within education. No longer was a handicapped person limited to being "crippled" or "retarded." Emotional, behavioral, and learning problems became legitimate disability categories.

Through the last decades of the twentieth century, those involved with educational research, coupled with teachers and parents giving their opinions, gave serious consideration to examining why some students who couldn't read, write, or do arithmetic were "smart" in other ways. People started looking for reasons for this phenomenon, and, as has happened throughout history, they found plausible answers. "Hidden handicaps" came to the fore.

To describe their findings, terms such as "learning disability," "emotional disability," and "behavioral disability" were coined and eventually added to the established list of conditions (e.g., blindness and deafness). Other long-standing conditions such as autism and traumatic brain injury were also included on the official register of impairments. Finally, the category "other health impaired" (OHI), perhaps the most nebulous of all, made the cut.

Although some of these conditions were ill-defined, often of unknown etiology, and absent any standard instructional regimen, they were put into law nevertheless. Schools could no longer systematically exclude disabled kids. To address the additional responsibility this engendered for educators, the search went out for solutions.

Those of us who were there at the beginning recall a sense of adventure. Teachers had the thrill of forging new territory and faith that a fresh educational landscape was being created. With the influx of special education came those with claims of gnostic insight that would fix all that ailed the disabled student. But, repeatedly, these secret remedies dissipated, leaving kids back at square one at best.

Special education has now had several decades to mature. The glitz is now gone and a time for settling in has come. Although problems never contemplated by those who drafted the special education legislation have become commonplace, two long-standing enigmas continue.

The first is comprehending the myriad of procedures codified in the law; the second is figuring out how to teach the kids. What remains consistent are the fundamentals that govern both the legal process and the principles of learning.

Meetings: A Microcosm of Special Education

A primary presumption in special education is that meetings will be conducted in good faith by knowledgeable people who are aware of and follow the rules. However, given the complications of special education, any number of variables can alter this basic plan. Of the several thousand individualized education plan (IEP) meetings I have been involved with over my career, the following are among the most memorable:

The biggest surprise ending: A student was arrested at the end of the meeting for threatening the vice principal with a paper clip. The administrator stated that this placed her in jeopardy of bodily harm. Whereupon the police were called, who handcuffed the kid and took him into custody.

The least conventional location: An IEP meeting had been scheduled for an especially recalcitrant student, and he had been requested to attend. Not surprisingly, when the meeting time arrived, the student was still in bed. No problem. The mom said she would make a pot of coffee, the IEP team drove to the house, and the meeting was held around the kid's bed while he stayed under the covers.

The most contentious: In one especially tense situation, both parents had restraining orders and were not to be within five hundred feet of each other. However, each rejected the suggestion to participate via conference call and demanded to attend the actual meeting. To "accommodate" this situation, the meeting was held in a room with a window in the door. Two police officers were stationed outside (they could not be in the room because of confidentiality issues), where they guarded the entire proceeding.

The longest: Thirty-four hours, involving several sessions spanning two months. The longest single session lasted nearly nine hours.

The shortest: Five minutes, thirty-four seconds. All participants had seen a draft of the plan, said there were no questions, and that was it.

The most culinary: To accommodate a parent's work schedule and teachers who had to work late, we had a pizza party during the meeting. The school provided the pizza and the parents brought a homemade dessert.

The most-exaggerated legal issue: When a meeting had to be moved to a different classroom to accommodate another group, the parent filed a complaint with the state Department of Public Instruction because he had not been provided with prior written notice of this change.

The saddest: A required annual meeting was held for a terminally ill student. We all knew this would be the last one. There were no dry eyes when the meeting ended.

The most participants: Thirty-nine, including teachers, related-services staff, therapists, and those invited by the parents. The meeting was held in a classroom, and someone walking by might have mistaken the group for a political action committee.

The most annoying: At a meeting to determine if a student's expellable behavior was a manifestation of his disability, the parent's advocate grabbed my note copy; wrote, "The student's behavior is related to his disability," so the kid could avoid expulsion; and said, "Now it's in the written record, so you can't do anything to him."

The least informed advocate: At one especially sensitive meeting, the grandmother of a high school girl who was pretty much unwilling to follow any school rules announced that she knew all about IEP meetings and would be the local education agency (LEA—i.e., school district) representative. It was somewhat satisfying to inform her that the LEA representative had to be an employee of the district, which she was not.

These meetings have some unique characteristics; however, and unfortunately, they are representative of situations that are far from rare. The team meeting is at the heart of special education procedure. It is serious business to be determining a student's status and educational services. To a significant degree, this meeting influences the direction for a disabled kid's life, and therefore it behooves all participants to take their responsibilities seriously and to actually know what they are supposed to be doing.

"The Drift Effect"

PROBLEMS IN SPECIAL EDUCATION ARE ALL TOO COMMON because of a "drift effect" that has occurred over time. Meanings of specific education terms and practices evolve and take on the shape of community values. A "poor reader" in one situation becomes a "dyslexic" in another. An impoverished kid from an unstable home may be considered a "hyper, off-the-wall little brat," whereas the same behaviors would be indicative of "a child with attentional and concentrational concerns" for a student from an affluent family. Such thinking is elitism at its best.

When disability law was first being formulated, impairment conditions were fairly visible and few, and not a lot of diagnostic information was needed. As indelicate as it may seem, the common thought was that handicapped people "looked" or at least "acted" disabled, and they stayed that way. Certainly some were misdiagnosed, but as foreign as it may now seem, there was little thought that instructional intervention would make much of a difference.

There was also an influence from the legal arena. With the advent of the civil rights movement and its focus on antidiscrimination and protection of individual liberties—even for school-aged kids—the way schools did business substantially changed.

Back to the Future—Kind Of

In 1969, teachers were faced with an ominous task. In that year the Supreme Court made the decision *(Tinker v. Des Moines Public Schools)* that schools had to consider students' constitutional rights—especially in the arena of freedom of expression and discipline. Some educators thought that adult authority, the previous basis of control, had crumbled. Many reasoned that, if order in the schools were to be maintained, they would have to find something to replace what they felt the Supreme Court had taken away.

Concurrently, attention was being paid to the often-wholesale discrimination against disabled students by schools. For many of those with handicaps, educational opportunity was significantly restricted; for others it was eliminated altogether. Within a few years after the momentous *Tinker* decision, federal special education laws were enacted. Schools could no longer disregard students with disabilities. The educational system was now held accountable to find ways not only to keep special needs students in school, but also to ensure they would be successful.

To address this perceived crisis, educators looked for a ready solution. The timing was ripe to apply methodologies based on available animal research. Since operant conditioning worked on pigeons, rats, and chickens, it was reasoned that it could be made to work on kids (though it was conceded that, if these strategies were to be used on students, they would need to be intensified or refined—even disabled kids would not work very long for food pellets and trinkets). But the concept seemed at least worth consideration.

Subsequently, behavior modification and programmed learning became dogma for many. A number of educators believed they now had hope of meeting the mandates being imposed on them by law, and many new instructional programs claiming they could make everything right again became commercially available.

Eventually, the limitations of these strategies came to the fore, but at that time there was precious little else for educators to latch on to. B. F. Skinner was looked on by many as some kind of messianic bringer of hope. Sequence, structure, and schedules of reinforcement became a triune focus. The premise emerged that any behavior, including academic skill, was considered fair game.

Politically, the idea arose that education had finally found its Rosetta stone. All educational problems were now presumed correctable, at least in theory. Philosophical statements like "All children can learn" morphed into "All children can succeed" and were adopted without much question. In fact, to say otherwise became a form of educational blasphemy.

Armed with the thought that schools should now be equal to the task, legislatures and courts increasingly developed specific mandates that exceeded the knowledge-base of individual teachers, if not the whole of education. The thought of many teachers was that when they finally knew what to do, a new dictum emerged. Education found itself perpetually trying to "catch its balance." A cycle had begun that would continue to spin for some time.

When the (Legal) Left Hand Doesn't Know What the (Educational) Right Hand Is Doing

Foundational to the problems in special education is that two different disciplines are the primary players. Those drafting the rules were primarily lawyers; those implementing them were primarily educators.

Generally, the legal and educational communities have little experience with each other's thought processes. Even when the same words are used, there is more than likely a different nuance. Words like "benefit," "disability," "education," "appropriate," and "need" are often interpreted from the perspective of the reader's experience rather than based on what may have been the original intention of the writer. This divergence in understanding gives ample opportunity to drift away from what those drafting the words actually meant. Eventually, those in the trenches end up working with what are really translations of translations of translations, in which the original concepts have become, at best, a bit distorted.

The honest fact is, if all sides were to have a working knowledge, or at least a respect, of each other's role in the special education process, everyone would be much better off. Essentially, there are a few foundational ideas that, if observed, will provide those involved in the education of special needs students with enough knowledge to avoid violating basic legal principles:

Special education protects due process rights. Special education is commonly considered a list of services a particular student is receiving beyond what is being provided to others. However, this is a fundamental misconception that disrupts the very process. Special education procedures have importance because every time an action is imposed on the basis of a disability, the student is increasingly separated from "being normal." And being normal is actually the fundamental right. The documents identifying instructional services (e.g., an IEP), then, are more than just cumbersome paperwork—they are actually records detailing that the student's due process rights have been observed.

The ultimate goal of special education is quite simple: getting kids ready for life when school is gone. There may be more delicate or professional ways to say this (e.g., "independence and employability"), but the meaning is essentially the same. Since this is the goal, it should be the basis of services provided throughout the student's special education experience.

Disabled students are in really, really bad shape. In the evolution of any movement, there is commonly some regression toward the mean. This is no less true of special education. Because of the legal nature of special education, many aspects are validated by process rather than by definition. For instance, the overwhelming presumption is that the conclusions of a duly formed team are correct. This presumption is further based on the concept that conclusions will be made within the parameters of law. However, as things have turned out, this is more of a wish than a hard-core reality. How can educators remain true to an original intent if there is little direct knowledge of what this original intent was?

The history of special education is replete with misdiagnoses, sometimes to the point of class-action suits and major changes in state law. At local levels, innumerable students have been placed in special education programs when what they really needed was a dose of all-around good teaching. Kids are placed in special education with pseudo qualifying language such as "struggle," "has difficulty with," and "occasionally."

There has been a tremendous influx of kids into special education for all sorts of reasons. When the system is abused, the whole process suffers and is mocked. Some consider having a disability very like having a badge of courage. Others hold the view that a kid may derive some advantage by being declared handicapped. For some, disability may even be a way to explain away personal faults, weaknesses, or guilt. Maybe these students will get additional help in school, be provided accommodations on college entrance tests, or qualify for some government-issued income, but to use the special education process for such ends violates its very purpose.

"Special education" is supposed to be special. Another issue is the tendency for people to find what they are comfortable with and just try to stay there. I recall one teacher from my years as a department chair. She was a pervasively unhappy reading teacher whom I suspect got her certification in learning disabilities so she could have a reduced case load and increased job security. Although the category of learning disabilities involves a number of academic skills, this teacher continued to teach reading. That was it. No math, no writing, nothing else. And she only taught one way: She had kids type words on index cards. I still remember her calling—as she seldom left the room—to order more cards and typewriter ribbons (this story occurred before the computer age).

The inappropriateness of this teacher's instructional scope is fairly apparent. More subtle are methodologies that have a research base, published curriculum, established name, and loyal following. Sometimes these specific methodologies are a false hope, sometimes they are an expectant wish, and sometimes they are right on target. Systematic inquiry is wonderful and a valuable asset in education, but the really valuable findings are those that remain after having percolated through the filters of time and common sense.

Special education is essentially customized instruction to address characteristics resulting from an individual student's disability and is analogous to tailor-made clothes, made-to-order kitchen cabinets, or anything else that is designed from a set of specifications. The contribution of special education teachers is their skill in creating individualized curricula or in devising strategies to meet individual needs. Falling into a comfort zone of one methodology is the death knell for effective teaching: It ignites burnout and substantially violates the individualization principle.

Any instruction or service provided through special education is to be individualized. As a result, there are no precedents in special education, and services are not necessarily restricted by currently available resources. This is not to say that special education is any kind of wish list or that the sky is the limit, but that provisions for special needs students are to be based squarely on what is identified by a team as an individual need resulting from the student's disability.

Within special education, instruction is to be based on a concept that is sometimes forgotten: The disability-related problems are to be either fixed or compensated for to orient the student to independence in adulthood. Of course, there will be innate limitations to be considered, but consistent prompting is needed in order to strive toward this goal and get beyond either day-to-day maintenance or crisis intervention.

I recall a meeting with a group of teachers regarding a kid whose behavior had significantly deteriorated because of a medication glitch. Based on the discussion with the special education staff, it was apparent the teachers were well versed in what to do after the kid misbehaved. However, in response to a question about what the teachers knew in terms of prevention strategies, the teacher in charge of behavior brought her index finger and thumb almost together but not quite touching and said, "About this much."

When working with special needs kids, there will always be situations that challenge our professional intellect. The question, however, is what action to take when an answer is not readily apparent. It seems some believe that if they don't already know what to do, there is little obligation to search for additional knowledge. This is not good.

In Special Education, Dumb Can Be Just as Powerful as Smart

WANT TO HEAR A SCARY THOUGHT? Decisions made by legally constituted special education teams are the most authoritative in the district. Whether correct or not, these decisions supersede board policy, established district procedures, employment master agreements, and individual philosophies. Whether accurate or not, the presumption of the law is that these teams will make decisions in conformity with the legal intent. This process is facilitated if everyone has a working knowledge of the procedural requirements involved. However, at the same time that educators are encouraged to remain current in their professional field, it is recognized that doing so is a herculean task.

Fortunately, there are some general principles underlying special education that facilitate sound legal and educational practices. If these foundational ideas are not observed, decisions of school-based teams, although perhaps logical and sincere, risk procedural and substantive flaws that can result in false diagnoses and corrective actions that are potentially time-consuming and expensive.

When Things Start Bad, They End Worse

As a high school sophomore, a student had been identified as eligible for services under Section 504 of the Rehabilitation Act of 1973. An individualized plan had been developed (that actually identified mostly what the teachers would do), filed away (neither the teachers nor the parents received a copy), and evidently forgotten.

Forgotten, that is, until the parents threatened legal action. Because of this young man's lack of school performance, his grade point average was below what his school required for him to be eligible to participate in sports. His parents claimed the problem was solely due to the fact that the teachers were not implementing his educational plan as developed the previous year.

The parents were in fact correct about the plan not being followed. Of the student's eleven teachers, only three were aware that there was a plan, and only one of them was implementing even parts of it. The potential legal liability to the district prompted a thorough review. As a result, it was discovered that the process for this student had been flawed from the onset.

Because the parents had initiated the legal action, the first contact was with them. Information obtained from a fifteen-minute call revealed that what happened was more like a script from the *Three Stooges* than a special education evaluation, and that a "dope slap" was well in order.

This whole debacle started with the parents contacting the school psychologist almost a year before a request for a special education evaluation had been made. The primary reason put forth by the parents was because their son was failing a number of classes. The parents emphasized at that time that they were not interested in a special education evaluation—just some simple testing would do.

The psychologist, outside any formal referral process (with its procedural accountability), administered a single test. From the results of that lone, disputable test, the psychologist declared that the student had "concentrational and attentional" problems.

Armed with this professional opinion, the parents went to their medical doctor. The doctor, who admittedly had little knowledge in the area of attention deficit disorder (ADD), wanted an "expert" opinion and recommended another person for the parents to meet.

The "expert," however, did no further assessment. Rather, she "reviewed" information provided by the school psychologist and parent and, with no further substantiation, summarily proclaimed that the student had ADD. This "verification" was then sent to the doctor, who, without further assessment, prescribed medication. So far, the only "evaluation" involved the results from one disputable test administered by the school psychologist, some months prior, to an adolescent who was disgruntled with school, at odds with his parents, and involved with kids for whom "wholesome" was not a descriptor.

At this point the parents referred the student for a special education evaluation. The team, headed by the same school psychologist who administered the only test given in this whole scenario, was presented with a diagnosis of ADD in a memo on a doctor's letterhead. The team also verified that the student was not doing well in school (which was true) and—bingo—the student was declared disabled. Interestingly enough, less than a year after the student had been "diagnosed," he was expelled from school for selling his medication (which he never took) to other students!

I can still recall the father cursing and throwing a pencil at the kid when the expulsion meeting ended. The parents' ploy to keep their son in sports by using the special education system to circumvent the grade policy eventually failed, and at a pretty hefty cost.

What a mess—and all largely because of a deviation from what should be standard practice. If this team would have done what they should, they would have avoided being duped and, just perhaps, the outcome for this kid and his parents would have been better. The role of procedure in special education is there for a reason. Those working with special needs students do not have to be lawyers, but it is so helpful if they know fundamental principles of the process.

The unfortunate reality is that special education is ripe for conflict between parents and schools. Decisions in special education are made by a group of people who exemplify a "different role, equal status" concept. That is, each member is expected to fulfill a particular niche for which they are qualified. When presenting information to be considered by the whole team, each member is to have commensurate standing. To a large degree, decisions are expected to be made without a boss.

Translating Procedure into Everyday Language

CERTAINLY, PROCEDURE IS NOT THE END-ALL AND BE-ALL of special education. However, when there are problems in the process, it is difficult for the other aspects (e.g., services, methodology, parent involvement, etc.) to function. It amazes me how often problems would be avoided by following a relatively few fundamental and commonsense principles:

1. *Be sure paperwork is done correctly, completely, and on time.* Failure to meet notice, consent, or collaboration requirements is among the best ways to come up short and likely lose in a case that goes to hearing. Last-minute requests for parent permission or hastily convened meetings only indicate the possible presence of other incompetencies. I remember a lawyer who represented parents making the statement that he had never lost a case in which the parents had not been properly noticed of actions anticipated by the district. It was his most efficient test to determine whether he would win.

2. ***Require members of the team be present throughout formal meetings.*** If all required district staff members are not in attendance for the entire time their input is part of the process, this is not a legally constituted team. In the event that a member is absent because of some unavoidable circumstance, a decision should be made at the onset of the meeting whether to continue or to postpone. With very few exceptions, if any district member of the team is absent, the meeting may be discontinued by any present member, including the parent.

3. ***Make certain documentation sufficient to justify all decisions is brought to the meeting.*** Professional judgment is not a guess, a feeling, intuition, an "I think" assumption, a ploy to avoid looking incompetent, a justification for stopping at "We don't know," or a decision made contrary to the data. All information on which decisions are made should be quantifiable, and there is no provision that the quest for answers should be ended because of a current lack of knowledge. Although teams are not responsible for discovering something that doesn't exist, they are responsible for eligibility, programming, and placement determinations that require high levels of professional expertise based on information obtained from objective evaluation.

4 ***Do what you say you will.*** Although putting a plan into writing and then not doing it may be common practice, it should not be. It is far better to have a conservative program that is actually implemented than an ambitious one that isn't. There are few situations more awkward than being at an annual review only to then find out that a plan had not been successful or that a kid had made insignificant progress. To a degree, written plans are a variant of "truth in advertising" and identify what and how much service will be provided to the student.

5. ***See to it that nobody stays confused for very long.*** Use wording that is free of nomenclature and understood by parents and other noneducators participating on the team. Formal meetings during

which the focus is on a kid's abnormalities can be an overwhelming experience for parents and others for whom special education is not just their job. Using expressions such as "standard score" or "regression formula" may give some a heightened sense of intellectual specificity, but it is gibberish to most. Even common words like "average," "significant," and "grade equivalent" take on cryptic meanings within a special education context. A sound practice is always to confer with parents and other members of the team in a follow-up "debriefing" before the process is considered complete.

6. *Consider input from all participants.* Although final decisions are made by the educational agency, input from all participants is to be part of the information considered by the team. When determining a student's current performance, identifying appropriate services, and deciding where the student will go to school, a collaborative approach is mandated.

7. *Stay focused on educational problems actually caused by the disability.* Goals and subsequent services should be related to addressing issues caused by the student's disability. This requires the team to identify the characteristics of the student's impairment that are causing the educational problems. Instruction and supports are to be designed to address the performance deficits being caused by the disability. To adhere to these parameters requires adequate evaluation information and a conscious effort from the team to stay on task. A related issue is that services should not be categorically driven. Once a student is identified as being eligible for services, the impairment label (e.g., "learning disabled," "emotionally disabled," "other health impaired," etc.) will have little place in subsequent discussion.

8. *Make certain there is internal consistency in both the process and the documents created.* There is to be a congruence in the process from the time a student is first considered for special help, to the final decision of the team. Therefore, information in a referral directs the evaluations used. Subsequently, a determination of eligibility must

be consistent with evaluation information. Likewise, programming and placement of eligible students must be based on information contained in the assessment identifying the characteristics of the disability that are causing the performance deficits that, in turn, caused someone to refer the kid in the first place.

9. *Be sure everyone is using the same yardstick when identifying levels of progress and amounts of services that will be provided.* One of the cardinal requirements of special education is that the skills and knowledge that disabled students are expected to attain be described in measurable terms. In a sense, writing goals for a disabled student is analogous to buying a plane ticket. If I were to call an airline and say that I wanted to go somewhere, sometime, on one of their planes, I would be quickly told I had given insufficient information. However, this is what often happens in special education documents. How often has "increase reading comprehension" been written with no clue as to the kid's comprehension level at the time the goal was written, or to what would constitute "increase"? There must be an end result that is measurable. This doesn't always mean that a normed-referenced score is identified. What it does mean is that no one on the team wonders if the student accomplished the goal.

10. *Say "no" by saying "yes" to something else.* When school staff state that a service for a disabled student will not be provided because of tight schedules, a tight budget, or just a "We don't do that here," I doubt if they know the liability they have just created. A cardinal rule is that services are not to be limited by resources. This is not to say that alternatives, based even on cost, cannot be considered, but that each alternative needs to provide the outcome for the student as determined appropriate by the team. Many a staff member has stood, hat in hand, before the tribunal to explain an expensive decision caused by a lack of knowledge, parental pressure, or a slip-up in procedure. I know from experience that this is not a comfortable place to be.

The key to avoiding this particularly uncomfortable trap is to find out what the purpose of any particular request stems from. Many times, the basis of the request is legitimate. However, when a request diverts from the ultimate goal of "independence and employability," it becomes difficult at best to justify. Sometimes people want an IEP to dictate what other people should do. I remember a father and mother wanting twenty of their daughter's classmates to be assigned to form a reciprocal friendship group just for her. That request was altered to providing the disabled student with instruction in social skills so she could develop her own relationships rather than have other kids assigned as friends (which, by the way, would have been a disaster).

Admittedly, there are a plethora of factors to be considered in complying with procedural and substantive appropriateness. However, observing these ten guidelines will significantly increase the odds that the process will work for most of the people, most of the time.

Balancing the Important Factors

WITHOUT UNDEREMPHASIZING THE ROLE OF PROCEDURE, it must be recognized that without consideration of the affective needs of those involved, the process can become little more than a bitter experience. Unless there is a recognition that teachers, parents, and kids are often hurting, confused, or both, the natural inclination will be toward self-preservation and mistrust. I close this chapter with a story about an especially sensitive meeting that demonstrates the importance of balancing legal requirements with the emotional needs of everyone involved.

Cory's Get-Together

Some years ago I was involved with a team for a student who had multiple disabilities, including hearing, cognitive, and medical issues. At the meeting, one of the staff suggested a goal that Cory would "attend to a task for thirty seconds, in one out of five sampled observations." That about blew my mind. That meant he could fail four out of five times and still be considered successful! A second goal submitted was for Cory to lift three pounds five times. A wonderful skill, perhaps, but to what end?

With the greatest of tact, I asked about the rationale for the first goal. I was concerned that such diluted learning would be insufficient to form a foundation for any long-term educational benefit. By analogy, I suggested, think of what might be acceptably mastered at this level for teachers. Would it be okay to learn the names of twenty percent of the kids, grade one-fifth of their papers, or only show up for work one day a week?

At this point, many of the staff firmly entrenched their defenses. Mostly, there was silence. One person pursed her lips (for the rest of the meeting actually), and I got "the look" from a couple others. The solid majority of the team were thoroughly irritated with me. I was an outsider (I was subsequently referred to as a "newbie" in one communication). However, decisions needed to be made by consensus, and I knew full well I would have to use my very best Love and Logic if the necessary levels of agreement were to be reached.

Realizing that the next interaction would influence the rest of the meeting, my opening comments, chosen with great care, were as follows:

David: "I have an idea, but I want you to know something first. I don't have a lot of social grace, so I don't embarrass easily. People can be very frank and honest with me, and I just don't have the inclination to take offense. Also, I don't have much of an ego. As result, I don't have a lot to get defensive about.

As my ideas are presented, if you think they are wrong, stupid, or inappropriate, you are free to say so publicly without any fear of hurting my feelings or even getting me upset. I'm weird that way, but that's just how I am. So, can I be assured that you will tell me right away if I make a mistake so we can all stay together?"

Since most meetings don't start this way, understandably the responses were tentative. However, there were no overtly negative reactions, so the conversation continued. (By the way, situations such as these provide opportunities for very practical application of interaction dynamics based on the Four Key Principles.)

"The purpose of what we are all doing is to get Cory ready for his life as an adult. Since he will be eighteen in a couple of days, we only have about three years left. I'm an adult and what I mainly do is work, play, and live. That about does it for me, how about you guys?"

There was cautious affirmation from the group, but I think mainly they were still not wanting to get suckered into anything.

"That's what I'm thinking about for Cory, too. He's going to live, work, and play. Does it seem reasonable that's what we should be getting him ready for?"

Eventually, we were able to come to agreement and developed an educational plan with a heavy emphasis on transition skills that Cory would need as an adult. This was a specialized school dealing with students at the severe end of the special education continuum, and the teachers were seasoned veterans. Yet the development and implementation of a formal written plan seemed to be little more than a laborious exercise that was only being done because some law required it.

Remedying the reluctance to observe sound practices requires an understanding of the system in a way that makes sense even to those who have somewhat of a disdain for procedure. However, when either procedural aspects of special education or people's emotional needs are disregarded, the process designed to benefit disabled kids becomes ripe for failure.

Chapter 4

The Other Side
of Achievement

How can we provide opportunities and rewards
for every degree of ability so that individuals
at every level will realize their full potentialities,
perform at their best and harbor no
resentment toward any other level?

— JOHN GARDNER

Know Anybody Who Wants to Do Bad in School?

IN OVER THREE DECADES AS AN EDUCATOR, every kid I can recall started their school career wanting to do well. A problem, however, is that what a lot of kids want, they cannot get. And when what kids want continues to elude them because the demands of school assault vital aspects of their personhood, they make every attempt to protect what sense of self-worth and control they feel is left.

In the process, it is quite easy for others to interpret kids' compensatory behavior as unreasonable, annoying, destructive, exasperating, or any other description one might use to mean "maladaptive." Actually, it is probably a misconception that recalcitrant students do not achieve anything—even apathy takes some doing. What is more accurate is that students are not attaining what is intended or desired by the adults.

Educational methodology, curriculum, class size, and technology have been studied over the past several decades in a sincere attempt to find the factors that are critical to success with these hard-to-reach kids. Some programs have stayed, some have evolved, and some have gone, who knows where. However, none of these attempts have been very effective on a long-term basis unless kids derive some internalized satisfaction from their participation. Otherwise, there is a strong tendency for kids to engage in failure-avoiding actions, challenge boundaries, act as though they perceive little or no purpose in what they are expected to learn, and waste their energies on emotional reactions. This tends to render even the best methodology, curriculum, and technology relatively moot.

For lack of a better word, how students "feel" about their education is a significant factor in how they engage in tasks that are part of the normal school expectations. In essence, if formal learning violates some fundamental need, many students will reject what is associated with it.

Thank God for Fs

Just as school is a good place for kids to learn, it is also a place ripe to develop and practice behaviors that can significantly mess them up. Any number of teachers and parents have wondered why certain students don't work to their potential and waste the opportunity to gain a competent education.

Some kids do so because they know how to use the system to obtain a particular goal. I recall one student who repeatedly said he was on the "D" (for "diploma") track. At any given time during the grading period, he knew precisely where he was relative to passing—and stayed ahead of the game just enough to avoid failing. His sophistication and rationale were really rather polished. He had identified his goal, knew what was needed to obtain it, and pursued it to completion.

Many other kids, however, seem to sabotage their educational careers into oblivion. They fail abysmally in spite of the fact that success could be theirs if they would only try. Homework is not done, let alone handed in, a mockery is made of tests, and class participation is counterproductive. One student, for instance, when given a "bubble form," filled in the little circles to compose the message "tests suck." The creative part was that he did it in mirror image.

For this student and countless others, there is a quandary: Why do they sometimes seemingly reject the educational opportunities afforded to them? Certainly there are legitimate concerns about appropriate curriculum and effective strategies, but beyond that, why do so many kids seem to fail on purpose?

For many, the answer is that they are desperately trying to protect those parts of their personhood they believe are under attack. In this quest, actually, Fs can be their salvation, because an F is about the only grade that can be obtained that will allow one to avoid a label reflecting lack of ability.

Kids can easily attribute their Fs to the teacher not liking them, the stupidity of the class, or other such external reasons that have a common characteristic: A sense of personal worth and autonomy are protected. Notice, it is a "sense of," not necessarily the real thing. But fooling themselves in this way is generally enough to get these kids through the day. To better understand the dynamics that maintain these behaviors, we need to go back to the very first year of life.

How We Connect

YEARS AGO I LEARNED ABOUT A MODEL from Dr. Foster Cline that explained the dynamics of how trust is developed in humans. There are several terms used when describing this cycle (e.g., *trust, bonding, attachment*), but they all refer to how human beings come to be connected with other people and values.

Normally, babies emerge from the womb as a cute bundle of needs with very little concern about how inconvenient getting those needs met might be to others. No baby I know apologizes for getting Mom up at two o'clock every morning to snack. However, if all goes generally well, by the time the child is a year or so old, basic cause/effect learning has resulted in trust and bonding with others—the essential elements of personal relationship and societal cohesiveness. The child is also progressing from mostly physical needs to those in the category of affective needs—self-concept and autonomy, to name just a couple.

This First-Year-of-Life Bonding Cycle is a quite simple model that represents how we form attachments to something outside ourselves. This model also allows us to extrapolate any number of applications that involve forming affinities—whether positive or otherwise. This process that explains why children come to love their parents and get excited about sports is the same process that explains why kids join gangs and vandalize schools. Simply put, we form attachments to whatever meets our needs, and we reject what doesn't.

First, let's look at a basic visual representation of the model:

The First-Year-of-Life Bonding Cycle

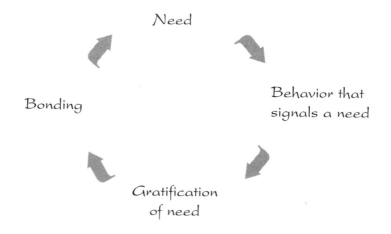

Need

Behavior that signals a need

Gratification of need

Bonding

Need: The cycle starts when there is a need, and as many of us know, infants are basically a bundle of needs. (My wife, Diane, and I took in dozens of preadoptive foster babies, and know this for an absolute fact!) If these needs aren't met, the infant will die, so their reaction to not having their needs met is pretty dramatic. It takes a hungry, frustrated baby little time at all to go from cute cooing to a full-blown hissy fit. This brings us to the second part: the emotional/behavioral reaction that makes the internal need very public.

Behavior that signals a need: If the infant's needs go unmet, a behavioral/emotional reaction is triggered. This reaction may start out fairly innocuous (e.g., fussing), but if unmet, a rage reaction soon results. Because the baby's needs are "survival" issues, the rage involves the baby's whole being. So a nurturing mother does not look at her raging infant and say, "Oh, my, you seem a bit out of sorts." Rather, she says, "Kid, you're throwing a real gold-medal fit right now." Rather than trying to simply stop the child's reaction (e.g., crying) with tactics that can range from bribes to abuse, the nurturing parent focuses on satisfying their underlying need.

Gratification of need: Adequate satisfaction of needs happens in a normally responsive environment with a healthy kid. But moving from the signaling of the need to gratification of the need is where things often go wrong. When the adult becomes frustrated and focuses only on the kid's emotional state rather than seeking to gratify the need, the cycle of developing trust and security becomes interrupted. If this is the consistent reaction of the adult and the kid succumbs, severe behavior problems may become locked in.

Bonding (trust, attachment, love, affiliation—and other concepts that require making connections): If the baby learns that expression of needs generally results in those needs being met, a sense of trust emerges. Sometimes the early environment does not at all meet a child's needs and this process is disrupted. Such is the case with abuse and neglect. At other times, however, the environment is normally giving, but unfortunately the child has a painful condition that neither the environment nor a loving mother or father can relieve.

Whatever the cause, this cycle breaks between the expression of the need and its gratification. And it's very understandable why this cycle can easily break, because so often when the kid is in an emotional state, so is the adult. Those under stress much more easily respond to the expression (e.g., crying, and in later life, whining, teasing siblings or classmates, oppositional behavior, etc.) rather than the need driving the kid's actions, which gets lost in the fray.

How Does This Relate to Achievement?

So, ONE MIGHT SAY THAT THIS EXPLORATION of connection is all well and good, but how does it apply to getting kids to stay involved with what they need to do in school? Although such factors as innate ability, relative difficulty of the task, and even luck are not to be discounted, the element of effort is a latent factor in student performance that has a global influence.

"Willingness": The Vital Part of Effort

Effort is not simply equated with how hard one might try to accomplish a task. In the context of our current discussion, there is also the concept of being willing to do what we *can*. Take driving within the speed limit, for example. Most people don't, even though it's within our ability to do so. Most drivers have the intellectual capacity to drive within the posted limits. They can read numbers and have sufficient physical coordination skills. So, for most drivers, adequate ability to achieve this task is presumably in place.

In addition, the task difficulty of driving within the limit is not inordinate. Again, the presumption is that if one has a driver's license, one is capable. Luck certainly plays a big part in this scenario. Most of the time that people speed, they get away with it. It is only the unfortunate few who get caught, and this doesn't happen consistently enough to bother most drivers.

But the effort part—now there is the crucial factor. If a driver is not willing (i.e., won't put forth the necessary effort) to drive within the posted limits, all of their intellectual ability, the doability of the task, and even luck will have little bearing. What kids decide to do in school follows this same pattern. Teachers are not so concerned with getting kids to exceed their capacity or skill levels. Rather, most people would be satisfied if kids simply did what they could. If this were the norm, books like the one you're reading now would likely be unnecessary.

Back to the Model

NOW BACK TO THE FIRST-YEAR-OF-LIFE BONDING CYCLE model. The basic premise is that we all have needs that are expressed in some kind of emotionally based behavioral response. When the need is gratified, then bonding locks in. However, if the cycle breaks before the need is gratified, the emotional/behavioral representation of that need is what remains.

Although the needs of an infant may be primarily physical, in a very short time a substantial transfer to psychological needs takes place. By the time a child is a couple years old, certainly by the time he or she is school-aged, the psychological needs often entirely diminish the physical needs. Kids will malnourish themselves to obtain approval, engage in risky activities to be accepted, and become a problem in school to protect their sense of well-being.

Here's How It Works

We all have needs, both physical and psychological. When there is a disruption in getting these needs satisfied, there is an emotional response. Imagine an infant. When well-nourished, dry, and occupied, we have a dear little bundle of joy. However, when any of these needs are not fulfilled, an emotional/behavioral response ensues. Likewise, for an older child, when an affective need is attacked by some element associated with school, problems arise. Within the paradigm of Love and Logic, and specifically applied to achievement issues, these psychological needs are represented by the Four Key Principles:

1. *Self-concept:* When students are confronted with classroom tasks they believe are beyond their ability (whether or not this perception is accurate), there is a sense of attack on personhood. In response, kids engage in self-protective behavior that can range from apathy to aggression—whatever it takes to divert attention away from personal deficits. When the need is satisfied, however, there is much more willingness to expend whatever effort is necessary to bring a task to completion (a fundamental component for school success).

2. *Shared control:* Because the very nature of school requires some curtailing of individual conduct, a key to effectiveness is setting parameters (e.g., rules) without making a problem worse. When kids have a sense that their autonomy is being attacked, they will fight to regain some control. If kids can't get back the control they think is rightfully theirs, they (like any of us, by the way) will substitute by controlling others, the environment, or both, in a number of ways, the most common being passive-aggressive/passive-resistive behavior (translated as, "I will do what you say, but not in the way you want it done"). However, when this sense of autonomy is satisfied, there is less reluctance to conform to parameters set by others.

3. *Empathy with consequence:* When confronted with lack of success, it is very hard to blame someone who is sincerely concerned (i.e., empathetic) with our plight. Those who show kids empathy (as opposed to pity, moralizing, or reminders) when they mess up also focus the offender on his or her behavior and how the ensuing outcomes affect them. As applied to achievement, when students understand that there is a direct and causal relationship between

what they do and the subsequent results, connections are internalized. Establishment of these patterns provides the stage for new learning to make more sense. What makes sense is more easily retained and forms a firm foundation for subsequent learning. Dependence on luck and discounting the value of what is being taught are diminished.

When there is a disruption in the patterns kids have developed to make sense of the world, they try to get back to the familiar and secure. Likewise, if kids perceive little purpose in what they are asked to do, engaging in the learning assigned by the teacher is not the normal outcome. However, when what is required does make sense and is associated with whatever has been previously accepted as valid, new learning is much more readily retained.

4. *Shared thinking:* When adults do the lion's share of the thinking, there is little reason for kids to be invested in the process. In addition, a common outcome is that kids pretty much accept that if the adult is worried about their problem, they don't have to be. This acceptance often rises almost to the level of faith, and students come to believe that the adults will keep really bad things (like flunking) from happening. Remember, whoever does the most thinking owns the problem, whoever owns the problem is expected to solve it, and whoever is the most invested also is blamable for any failure. When kids are allowed to practice thinking, they become much better at problem solving without being a problem to others. In neurological terms, they get "smarter" by growing more dendrites—a vital aspect of the learning process. We get better at what we practice.

Some Cautions

When classroom demands attack kids' psychological/affective needs, they essentially engage in behavior to protect themselves and survive (psychologically). What compounds the problem is that the adults often interpret the cause of the problem largely through their own perceptual set. The adults often become Godlike and declare what the problem kid is thinking, but such a declaration is essentially based on how the kid's behavior is affecting them. The trick for educators is to develop the professional skill of analyzing what need the student is attempting to meet rather than only reacting to the overt emotional response. This is hard, because we can't see the need, but we sure can see what the kid is doing that is ticking us off. This kind of thinking requires a much higher level of professional expertise than it takes to learn law, medicine, or engineering.

Needs are innate parts of the human psyche, and the manifestation of these needs is a fairly automatic reaction. So those two parts of the cycle are pretty much a given. When a need is gratified, there is a bonding to whatever did the gratifying. This is the scary part, because sometimes what or who does the gratifying is not all that wholesome.

The other part of the equation is that if the need is not gratified, it is the emotional/behavioral response that will become locked in. Although there are certainly some individual aspects to people's reactions to any given circumstance, the general outcome of an unmet need is that the emotional expression can easily rise to the level of being maladaptive.

What Can Teachers Do?

Decades ago, Ferdinand Hoppe described "sustained continuous achievement" as performance that is beyond current levels, yet obtainable through practice and effort. Hoppe also concluded that motivation to achieve remained persistent when progress was contingent on effort and practice. That is, when the variables for performance are directly under the influence of the individual, achievement is significantly increased because of motivation and engagement in the task.

This largely explains why many are more expert at a hobby than at their job. It also largely explains why so many students can recite, verbatim, esoteric trading-card facts, but can't remember enough to pass a test.

Through his research, Hoppe found that for students to remain engaged in the learning process, they need to have a feeling of success, irrespective of the performance of others. That is, when students feel a sense of personal satisfaction with their accomplishment, they have a higher level of willingness to maintain involvement in the task or activity. As a result, they increase their skill mastery, because they stay the course longer (i.e., time on task). The innate value of the activity is secondary to the subjective satisfaction that comes from completion. Isn't it interesting how research often identifies what is right in front of us and confirms what we already know? In addition, isn't it interesting how often we disregard the research?

Hoppe further established that a sense of satisfaction occurs from achievement when progress is measured on the basis of the person's own past performance, not in comparison to the accomplishments of someone else. When winning means being better than someone else, a win may bring an initial elation, but only to be replaced by an underlying dread that, at the next competition, the former winner may well become the future loser.

Very of often, in our educational system, having a difficult student is like a bad pregnancy. It's rough for nine months, but there is an end. As a result, there is a tendency for some teachers to tolerate kids for the duration rather than expending the effort necessary to resolve interpersonal problems. However, throughout history, whenever teachers have had some basic ideas, they've also had an uncanny ability to adapt those ideas to specific kids and situations. Following are ten representative actions for those who work with kids to consider:

1. Provide options for having students demonstrate skill mastery. Written tests are not the only way students can show what they know.

2. Concentrate on descriptive comments of student performance rather than judgmental responses. "You have written a whole paragraph"

can be more powerful than "You did a good job." Remember, we want a judgment to be made, but we want the kid to make it.

3. Define achievement as accomplishing a goal rather than being better than someone else. Normed-referenced/competitive achievement makes only the top ten percent feel good. Everyone else feels not good.

4. Provide wait time to allow students to process. Eleven seconds seems like an eternity, but it is a magic amount of time and the results will be phenomenal.

5. Anchor the student on success. Mastery levels of at least ninety percent are necessary to ensure that a foundation for further learning is established. Also, if tests and assignments are structured with questions sequenced from easy to difficult, kids will do more.

6. Do not rob the student of feeling both success and failure. Regardless of the structure of any system, students need to have opportunities to make decisions about what they learn, how they learn it, and how they will demonstrate what they learn.

7. Adopt a consequential grading system that reflects skill mastery rather than skill acquisition. "Busy work," practice, unrelated extra credit, and behavior have little place in reporting academic progress.

8. Model self-acceptance. There is nothing more powerful to a student than to see what their teacher does when he or she makes a mistake.

9. Remember, all misbehavior is a maladaptive way of getting a legitimate need met. For the most part, anything any of us do is focused on enhancing a sense of self-worth and avoiding a sense of failure.

10. Keep in mind that we are all different in degree, not in kind. We would react exactly how the kids do if we felt what they are feeling. The only thing different is what triggers the response.

Understanding the Role of Love and Logic

THE BASF CORPORATION HAS A SLOGAN that conceptualizes the role of Love and Logic: "We don't make a lot of the things you use. We make a lot of the things you use better." Curriculum, strategies, and methodologies are all acknowledged aspects of achievement. Those who work with kids, especially kids with special needs, have an obligation to maintain high levels of professional expertise. However, in the words of the writer of Ecclesiastes: "There is nothing new under the sun." The goal of education (and specified in federal special education law) is to get kids ready for the real world. To do so, students need to (1) believe in themselves, (2) work collaboratively with others, (3) understand causal relationships, and (4) use their intellect to solve problems. In brief, these are precisely the concepts embedded in the Four Key Principles of Love and Logic. See pages 12 to 14 for a description of these Key Principles.

Chapter 5

Responsibility:
The Final "R"

I am not taking the blame for anything.

— TIERNAN MOORE (AT AGE FIVE)

Out of the Mouths of Babes

SOME TIME AGO A COLLEAGUE WAS RELATING an early-morning story about getting ready to leave the house for work and school. Although this mom was often the cause of delays, on this particular day she was well ahead of schedule and was standing in the doorway, waiting for her kindergarten-aged son, who had yet to put on his shoes and socks. Somewhat pleased with herself, she took the opportunity to make brief mention that, today, lateness was not her fault.

The boy, perceptive beyond his years, realized he stood as the accused and was not about to take on this awesome liability. Being accountable for such cosmic mistakes as making the family late is a heavy burden—one not many of us are strong enough to accept readily.

In response to his mother's insinuation, he dropped his shoes and socks on the floor, made a dramatic downward slashing gesture with his hands as though to cut off any misconception, and expressed a statement that rings as a theme in our culture: "I am not taking the blame for *anything!*"

Avoiding responsibility is pandemic and was one of the earliest acts of humankind. Adam, when confronted with that first wrongdoing (eating the forbidden fruit) had an immediate excuse. Upon God's question (using the King James version of the Bible for sake of the classic language and offering a smattering of my own commentary in the brackets), "Hast thou eaten of the tree whereof I commanded thee that thou shouldest not eat?" Adam had a ready response that did not directly answer the question (in Love and Logic, we call that a "bird walk") and made a rather lame attempt at blaming someone else: "The woman, who [if you remember, by the way, was *your* idea, not mine] thou gavest to be with me, she [through no fault of my own, I remind you, again] gave me of the tree and I did eat."

Not only did Adam not want to take the blame, but he also basically insinuated that God, Himself, was responsible, because it was His decision in the first place to bring Eve into the picture. Regardless of theology, the point to be made is that not taking responsibility for one's own actions seems deeply rooted in the human experience.

There should be little surprise, then, that the societal penchant to avoid personal responsibility has saturated our educational system. In special education, especially, it is a short trip from attributing a behavior to a student's disability, to exempting that student from being accountable for any consequences. How many times have we heard a student say, "I can't behave because I have . . ." (complete the sentence with some condition, real or perceived). Just a few years ago, a student told me he didn't have to follow school rules because his doctor had said that he was bipolar. There is little doubt that those with disabilities may well have to work harder to attain certain aspects of personal development, but it is hardly in anyone's best interest to believe responsibility is unattainable.

That Ol' Self-Concept Keeps Rollin' On

WILLINGNESS TO BE RESPONSIBLE FOR ONE'S OWN BEHAVIOR is inextricably intertwined with self-concept. Blaming others just lets people fool themselves into feeling better, at least for the moment. Otherwise, they might have to admit they are a tad flawed. "Making the other guy wrong doesn't make me right" (a phrase from the work of Sally Ogden), and avoiding culpability may be only a temporary fix, but that's all right. A decent number of temporary fixes adds up to a pretty hefty total and is usually good enough for the time being.

Although a sophisticated psychological analysis might conclude that people would be more at peace with themselves if they accepted their weaknesses with magnanimity, this would take a mighty effort. Not unlike the Greeks of old, our society highly reveres physical and intellectual perfection. On the other hand, if people have even a slight suspicion they are hardly in either of those categories, significant mental energy will be exerted in the pursuit of protecting personhood.

So instilled is this concept that most everyone lives in a kind of perpetual fear of being wrong. In response, we develop a very refined skill of always having a ready justification for just about anything we do. Most of us have practiced so much that the response is pretty much automatic. If I can convince myself that any indiscretion or error on my part is not my fault, I can keep this terrible fear of being wrong (and thus defective) at arm's length.

Bad Lungs, Fat Thighs, and Economics

This penchant of ours to avoid responsibility is also supported by established social conventions. Some time ago I read that the United States was the most litigious country in the world, with about one lawsuit filed for every twelve people. I'm sure there are lots of legitimate cases, but I admit questioning the worthiness about suing for getting lung cancer when cigarettes are abused, becoming obese because too much fast food is eaten, or scalding body parts from spilling hot coffee.

Maybe a large part of the problem comes down to money. Just think of the devastating economic impact and political upheaval that would occur if exercising personal responsibility became the norm. Imagine, for just a moment, the significant effects: People would no longer be hiring tax lawyers to get them out of trouble, the number of psychotherapists would drop dramatically, and jobs would be lost because everyone would be putting in a full day's work for a full day's pay.

Even schools would be affected. In special education, only students with real disabilities—not those who have gotten into the system for ulterior motives—would be on the rolls. Energies now devoted to legal battles, demands of dysfunctional parents, efforts to improve ineffective teachers, and dealing with ornery kids could be focused on instruction.

However, accompanying the acceptance of responsibility is a plethora of offshoots to contend with: What will people think? Will there be a big-time cost to me? Is what I did really all that bad? These are but a few of the questions that flood our minds and complicate what may seem an easy call.

Choices and Decisions

BEING RESPONSIBLE IS A CHOICE. Certainly, there is an element of subjectivity—to be sure, we are all individuals. However, there are actually some fairly static and rigid aspects of why people make decisions. The Four Key Principles of Love and Logic provide a template for understanding why we accept or reject taking responsibility for our actions:

1. *Self-concept*: The double-edged sword of accepting responsibility for our own behavior is that we tend to engage in activities with the intent of enhancing our sense of self-worth. Conversely, we have a strong tendency to avoid what we believe will reflect badly on us.

Since failure is an efficient destroyer of self-concept, we make every effort (whether conscious or not) to interpret our actions in a way that we can feel validated even when things go awry. The ultimate self-deception is when, with confident assurance, we can pronounce what someone else is *really* thinking regardless of their actual words or actions.

Observe people's behavior when they are trying to increase their social status. Adolescent boys without nearly the wherewithal to be macho put on an act, thinking they are impressing the girls. Those with verbal insecurities mispronounce esoteric words or use them out of context in an attempt to impress others through vocabulary. Some who cannot otherwise win friends spend a good portion of their paychecks to buy rounds of drinks they can ill afford—all in a futile attempt to create a positive image. These people are motivated, to be sure, even though they may be simply fooling themselves.

So a very firm bottom line is that if there is any consideration on my part that taking responsibility for my actions will damage my self-concept, avoiding such a decision will seem of much more valuable personal benefit.

2. ***Shared control:*** People are generally willing to accept responsibility for what they acknowledge having some control over. The converse of this, however, is that it is fairly easy to decline being responsible for what they cannot control. As reasonable as this may seem, maneuvering a circumstance to demonstrate that a mistake is outside of a person's direct influence may well be a ploy for not accepting any responsibility for any part of the problem. After all, the reasoning goes, certainly no one could be held accountable for what might go wrong if they have no sovereignty over the very thing causing the problem.

This gives people quite a reason to not become overly conscientious about being involved. The more ignorant a person is of solutions and their power to influence circumstances, the safer they feel. And what can readily be accused besides the person involved? Anything that can be argued as being outside one's control. And what targets are always readily available? Bad luck is always an option, and if that fails, there is always society and the general circumstances of life. And for many (à la Adam), there is always God. Perhaps in the great beyond, there are many who are shocked to find out that God doesn't take kindly to taking the fall for people's unwise decisions.

3. **Empathy with consequence**: Everyone does what seems to make sense, even if it is a somewhat distorted sense. What accrues benefit or allows the avoidance of something unpleasant makes sense. If some action really isn't going to cost me a lot, why put a lot of effort into it? Kids who are enabled or bailed out have little reason to "own up" to their mistakes, because they seldom have the opportunity to develop a cause/effect association between their behavior and what (should) happen to them.

   It is fairly easy for just about anyone to make up their own rules. People determine what is to their best advantage, develop arguments to invalidate any contrary opinion, and that's it. When it comes to avoiding responsibility, finding evidence to exonerate ourselves from blame without disrupting some cosmic order is actually quite easy.

4. **Shared thinking**: If people acknowledge understanding the relationship between what they do and what has happened to them, they are much more likely to accept some responsibility for the result. However, if they don't (or better yet for them, can't) understand something, then, certainly, they cannot be responsible for any resulting outcomes.

   I recall a conversation with a school psychologist some years ago. A referral had gone awry because she had unilaterally decided that a student would not qualify for special education and that she was going to stop this "scam job" before it went any further. This was a very nonjudicious decision, but each time the topic returned to how her behavior had unnecessarily complicated the situation, resulting in an awkward legal involvement, she furrowed her brow, tilted her head, and said, "I can't understand what you are saying." I thought it was interesting that she said "can't" rather than "won't" or even "don't," but the intent was clear. As long as she couldn't understand what was being said, there was no impetus for her to accept the responsibility for her actions.

Rules or Values

WHEN SOMEONE IS DESCRIBED AS IRRESPONSIBLE, what is often meant is that the person is not following a set of standards preferred or prescribed by those in authority. Kids not doing their homework or employees padding their expense accounts are but two simple examples. In essence, they don't follow the "right" rules. But what about common instances when people do follow the rules — even those that seem pretty stringent, obtuse, or even contradictory to the apparent goal?

I am hardly a sports aficionado, but the whole arena of fan behavior is fascinating to me. Take, for instance, the childlike acceptance of football rules as though they were given through some divine pronouncement. For sure, there may be plenty of examples of disagreement with an official's call, but I have never heard of anyone publicly, even when emotions are running high, debauching or condemning the actual rule.

For instance, in the game of football, it would seem that if the goal is to get the hide of a dead pig from one end of a playing field to the other, rules against holding, unnecessary roughness, or other violations for which flags are thrown would have little rationale. However, the rules are tenaciously adhered to.

Conversely, I can think of any number of instances when rules are so commonly disregarded that violations become the norm: exceeding the speed limit, cheating on tax returns, and returning used items as if they were new, to name just a few. In a school context, the list of broken rules would be exhaustingly long.

So why are the rules followed in football and not in other venues? I think it is largely because those who choose to conform to any rules first accept the values that those rules represent. Football fans first accept sportsmanship and fair play as valid concepts, whereas taxpayers argue that the government has too much of their money already and drivers contend that speed limits are unnecessary restrictions on their freedoms.

The reality for football, for instance, is that getting the ball from one end of the field to the other is actually secondary to how that feat is accomplished. Following the rules of the game actually makes victory more valuable, because skill rather than just brute force can then prevail. Breaking the rules governing school, on the other hand, often brings status. For many, getting through a course by cheating is significantly preferred over being honest and failing. Plagiarism is justified because the assignment was stupid or unreasonable to begin with. If I don't know and accept the value generating a rule, I have little incentive to conform.

Teaching by Example

I FIRMLY BELIEVE THAT THE TRUTH about anything human is not so much encapsulated in esoteric research studies or in declarations of best practice. Rather, truth about people is best taught through stories that provide lessons that can benefit us all. As to examples of responsibility, there are surely the Mother Teresas and Abraham Lincolns, but we often need stories from people who are more like ourselves for learning to become locked in.

The following story was told by a participant in one of my classes and shows what happens when kids see fallible adults demonstrate personal responsibility for their actions when it really counts:

As a director of a residential home for delinquent boys, I often had calls from workers when things went wrong. One evening a resident had used up more than his share of his supervisor's patience. This student was angry and aggressive and on this particular day I decided I was done with him. Not only was this kid not going to have any more chances, I intended to vent every ounce of my anger on him.

When I got to the group home, I stomped in, raced to the kitchen (where the kid was at the time), and got to within inches of his face. I was mad and I was going to let this kid have it.

Then I was flat on my back on the floor. I still don't remember anything between my first intention to yell at this kid and looking up at him from where I ended up. He had clocked me real good.

As I lay on that floor, my first thought (being decked actually cleared my head) was that I was about to get the crap beaten out of me. Then I looked at the kid. There were tears streaming down his face. He knew I held absolute decision-making power about what would happen to him for the foreseeable future. What I was about to say was not scripted and, frankly, not all that eloquent.

My brain and mouth were directly connected as I said, "Has your day been as sh--ty as mine?" You see, I knew what had happened was my fault. This is not to excuse this student's behavior, but I recognized that when I so aggressively violated this kid's zone of safety, all he saw was his abusive dad and he struck out to protect himself.

"Want to talk?" I asked him. He sat on the floor with me and we spoke for over two hours. It was a great lesson for me, and for the rest of the time this student was with us, there were no other incidents.

The honest fact about responsibility is that it costs both those learning and those teaching, and sometimes this cost is significant. And truth be told, sometimes taking responsibility doesn't even feel good, but it is the right thing to do.

Owning and Solving Problems

BEFORE ANYONE CAN DEVELOP A SENSE OF RESPONSIBILITY, there must be a feeling of problem ownership. Because kids learn from an early age to shove the blame for their mistakes onto others, it is often necessary to engage in a specific process to get kids to a point of accepting responsibility for the problem they caused.

A specific strategy is the "Five-Part Process to Owning and Solving Problems." Although simple on its face, this process can be applied to any number of situations where kids have to be moved from denial, to acceptance of fault, and finally to a willingness to participate in the solution.

The five parts, summarized, are as follows:

1. *Start with an expression of empathy.* This gives kids the understanding that the adult is acknowledging their feelings without approving or condoning any that might be inappropriate. Example expressions of empathy would include: "Bummer," "Oh, man," "Bet that feels terrible," and other such phrases that establish legitimate sadness for the kid.

2. *Give an implied message of capability.* The importance of implied messages cannot be overestimated in this process. The intent is largely to change the kid's perception from that of blaming others to not only internalizing a sense of personal responsibility for one's action, but also becoming actively involved in devising a solution. Examples of implied messages of capability would include: "What are you going to do?" "How are you going to handle that?" and other words that suggest that the adult is confident the kid will be able to come up with an answer. Remember, if we believe someone is capable, we ask for their ideas. However, to people we believe lack the wherewithal to think, we tend to just dictate.

3. ***Gain permission to share alternatives.*** Since unsolicited advice is seldom heeded, we essentially get the kid's approval to go further. Also, notice that alternatives or options are shared—not solutions. Again, remember, we want the kid to be thinking hard about what can be done to rectify the problem. If the adult gives a solution, the process loses its effectiveness. Although there are any number of variations, the model question for this part is: "Would you like to hear what others have tried before?" Wording such as this does not threaten or lock kids into defensiveness, and usually appeals to their sense of curiosity.

4. ***Have the kid verbalize the consequences of each alternative.*** Once an alternative is presented, the question "How would that work out for you?" generally prompts kids to come up with an answer that makes sense to them.

5. ***Give the kid permission to solve or not solve the problem.*** This is actually the hardest for a lot of teachers and parents, because they would feel better if the kid came to closure immediately after the first four steps. However, kids need time to process, and if they truly own the problem, then it should be their prerogative to determine their next move.

Let's take a look at a kid named Matt and see these five steps in action. Matt had a long history of not doing any of his work. He was bright (intellectually gifted, actually), and could have been an honors student in passive-resistive behavior. Threats, promises, bribes, and even retention had not worked. This was a kid who desperately needed to have some ownership of his problem, but had been given precious little opportunity. There is a progression I often mention in presentations: "Whoever is most invested in the problem gets to own it; whoever owns the problem gets to solve it; and whoever comes up with a solution gets to be blamed for its failure." The (sincere) adults in Matt's life exemplified this to an extreme degree. Hundreds of hours were spent trying to figure out what to do to Matt, and each plan pretty much died from pure exhaustion.

I remember meeting with Matt one night after his baseball practice. The following script represents the conversation we had regarding the great danger that failure in some of his classes would cause—delay of his graduation date:

Adult: "Well, Matt, looks like things are not going well. My guess is, that doesn't feel real good. Have any idea what you might do?"

Note: Steps 1 and 2 are now complete, and it only took a few seconds.

Matt: "No."

Note: Here we must emphasize that it is the quality of the kid's response, not the quantity, that is important.

Adult: "I know your dad and a lot of teachers have tried lots of things that haven't worked out real well, and I only have a couple of other ideas left—would you be interested in hearing any of them?"

Matt: "Yeah."

Note: Although Matt is a very bright kid, he is not using all of his advanced verbal skills yet.

Adult: "Well, one idea would be to keep going like you are now and just see how things might go. How would that work out?"

Matt: "Not good. It's going to take me forever to get out of school if I keep failing."

Adult: "Yeah, but some kids I know take longer to get through high school. One kid took about six years. That's not forever, but how would that work out for you?"

Matt: "Not good. I want to get out of high school as fast as I can."

Adult: "Okay. Well, what about just doing enough to get by. You know, Ds will get you through."

Matt: "Yeah, but I want to go to college and I couldn't get into Madison [a state university campus] with grades that low."

Note: Because Matt is already getting low grades, this would have been a perfect opportunity to start moralizing and reasoning. However, such actions on the part of the adult would simply void the effectiveness of this strategy.

Adult: "Hmmm. Guess that probably is true. Matt, that's about all I can think of now. Any ideas?"

Matt: "I hate homework and I wish I could spend more time with my family. What if I ask the teachers to give me assignments for the whole week on Monday. I wouldn't mind working hard for three days if I knew I didn't have to do anything at home on Thursday and Friday."

Adult: "That sounds like a plan. Who would you have to talk with?"

Matt: "Hmmm. Mrs. O---- [the building administrator] and probably the teachers."

Adult: "Is there anything you want me to do?"

Matt: "You could be there when I talk with Mrs. O----, but not with the teachers."

Adult: "Matt, I'm impressed. Hope it works out. Call me when you have the meeting with Mrs. O---- set up."

Matt's solution was one that the adult would probably never have thought of. This whole scenario emphasizes the fact that if we want kids to be responsible, they have to be directly involved in the process. The frosting on the cake is that kids will often come up with solutions that address the problem and demonstrate encouragingly high levels of creative thinking.

Early the next school year, as I was walking down a hall in Matt's school on my way to meet with a teacher, someone grabbed my arm—it was Matt. He was all smiles as he said, "I'm getting mostly all As now. I have one C, but I know how to bring that up." What a turnaround for this kid. Certainly, there is the corporate influence of all those who cared for and worked with Matt. However, all of those sincere attempts were frustratingly ineffective until Matt, himself, took ownership of his decisions.

Four Steps to Responsibility

The basics of providing kids an opportunity to learn responsibility are essentially a matter of setting up an environment where cause/effect relationships do the teaching. Tempered with those aspects of individuals that make them unique (e.g., personality, experience, preferences, etc.), values are developed because they make sense to the individual and are worth whatever price is to be paid.

People will be more ready to take responsibility for their behavior if none of the Four Key Principles of Love and Logic are violated. It is a fairly easy task to take credit for actions that supply a person's need for validation or autonomy. The trick is to orient people toward having the same satisfaction when taking responsibility for mistakes. This can only be done in a context where it is safe to take risks and where others provide the same level of support regardless of circumstances.

One of the first "procedures" I learned when starting to use Love and Logic was the Four Steps to Teaching Responsibility. By my rendering, these four steps are as follows:

1.   Give a task the kid can handle.

2.   Expect that a mistake may be made.

3.   Let the consequences fall.

4.   Give the same responsibility again.

Now let's expand on each of these elements:

1. ***Give a task the kid can handle.*** It's certainly important to know what is developmentally appropriate for, or otherwise within the ability of, any kid. If we demand performance beyond what a person is capable of doing, so much effort will be expended to protect self-concept and a sense of autonomy that learning responsibility will fall by the wayside.

2. ***Expect that a mistake may be made.*** Whereas the first step requires an intellectual decision, the success of this second step is pretty much dependent on the attitude of the adult. If the goal is to prevent kids from messing up, and then they do mess up in spite of our valiant efforts, the adults get rather discombobulated and start to become more (emotionally) invested than the kid. How many have seen a kid mess up only to have an overinvolved adult come in to rescue or take over? Whatever else we can say about mistakes, they sure do get our attention. The key is not so much to prevent kids from making mistakes as it is to ensure that they will learn from them.

3. ***Let the consequences fall.*** This step involves the purest of psychology: cause and effect. And consequences, at their heart, are all about cause and effect. The problem for kids arises when adults interfere with this fairly natural process. I recall seeing one of my special education students doing some "overtime" in the hall during his lunch. He was serving a detention for not completing his homework. Although the concept of detention must have had some value to the teacher, it was of little "consequence" to the student. As the student expressed to me, eating his lunch alone, but in relative peace, was, hands down, a cheap price for getting out of doing an assignment he didn't like.

4. ***Give the same responsibility again.*** Imagine a coach saying to a player, "You didn't do very good in the game today, so you can't practice until you get better." Sounds ludicrous, doesn't it. How can

the player be expected to get better while being prohibited from working on skill development? But compare the coach's dictum to the following common pronouncements given to kids when they mess up:

"You can't go on any more field trips because you behave so badly."

"You two can't sit together ever again because you can't be trusted."

"You cheated—that's a zero and drops your report card grade to a solid F."

This does not mean we give kids chance upon chance. What it does mean is that embedded within this process is instruction. Just as a good coach would help an athlete improve by evaluating the problem and developing interventions, so too should a teacher when a kid misbehaves.

My Lesson from Jaben

I learned the value of the Four Steps to Teaching Responsibility from my son, Jaben. It was an expensive lesson for both of us, but one I have never forgotten.

For seventeen years, my wife, Diane, and I had taken in preadoptive foster babies and seldom had free weekends. On a rare occasion early one October, however, we did. Our kids were old enough to stay alone for a couple of days, and Diane and I took off for some alone time. Little did we know this was to be Step 1—Give a task the kids can handle.

When we returned home late Sunday night, both kids were sitting on the couch, watching television. After the normal "How did everything go?" questions, we unloaded the car. What should have been our first clue that something was wrong was when we couldn't find the dirty clothes hamper. Then there was the missing portable bathtub whirlpool (we'd never taken out of the box). And the list kept growing. Next was the missing wristwatch Diane's dad had given her when she was twenty-one, and the missing old gold pocketwatch that had been her grandfather's. As best we could eventually figure, over four thousand dollars' worth of stuff was missing.

In the four-step sequence, we are now at Step 2. It was a hard step. Expecting your kids to make a mistake is easy to do in theory. Reality, however, is sometimes quite unpleasant.

One of our very few "rules" had been broken. We had an understanding with our kids that, when we were gone, no other kids were to be on the property. This was a revision of a rule against having other kids in the house, which we changed when Jaben had justified to us once that, since the garage was not the house, it was acceptable for his band to practice there. I even remember him accentuating this justification by telling us he didn't even let any of his bandmates use the bathroom (come to think of it, he never did tell me what they *did* use).

Getting back to the original story, during that Saturday morning, Jaben came back to the house with a friend. He was just going to get something out of his room and, of course, letting his friend come into the house and get out of the cold would not be a problem. However, this friend found out the house would be adultless that night, and told a couple of his friends, who told a couple of their friends . . . As well as we can figure, there were nearly twenty unaccompanied teenagers in our house that night, the vast majority of whom Jaben did not know.

You can imagine how Diane and I, as parents, felt. Our kids knew better. Some of the stolen items were irreplaceable. We were angry and disappointed. But it had happened and couldn't be undone. On to Step 3.

Letting the consequences fall is not so easy. First, there is a natural inclination on the part of the parents to not want to see their children suffer. There is also the natural inclination on the part of the kids to not want to suffer. There is also a simultaneous feeling on the part of the parents to want to exact some significant penalty on their kids to balance the wrong they have committed. Thus the bind for loving adults and the necessity for them to go beyond their natural feelings.

A lot of stuff had been taken that Saturday night, including some money out of Jaben's billfold and his house key. He found out about the money when he came up empty-handed in trying to pay for a Big Mac. That was a good consequence. The house key also provided another opportunity.

Our house is pretty valuable to us, and now somebody of ill repute had a key. A reasonable option seemed to be to change the locks. So I went to our local home-improvement store and bought the very best locks they carried. They were also the most expensive, and guess who got to pay for them? Jaben, of course. It took about three weeks of his paper-route money to finance that little purchase.

Now although he paid for the locks, guess who didn't get a key? Jaben, of course. In addition to having lost some material things, we had also lost some trust. We told Jaben that, now that he didn't have a key, it might be in his best interest to tell us if he were not going to be home at an expected time, so he wouldn't be locked out. One day he didn't call, and as a result Jaben provided himself with another wonderful opportunity for Step 3 of the responsibility process.

Diane and I had decided to do some shopping. We didn't stop until the stores closed, and when we got home Jaben was there, huddled on the step by the front door. It was a typical Wisconsin November night. Jaben had been waiting for some time and was cold to the core.

It is times like these when the combination of empathy and consequence is especially validated. Jaben had already experienced the consequence—he didn't need lecturing or moralizing. Rather, we commiserated about how cold he must have been and suggested that some hot cocoa might feel good. He never got mad, because he knew that he was responsible for his condition. And on to Step 4—give the same responsibility again.

That Christmas, Jaben got an unusual present: a house key. This is where I learned my own lesson. Before this, Jaben had "lost" three keys, and I, not fully understanding how I was contributing to the problem, went to the hardware store and got him a replacement each time. Not the best example of good parenting.

When this story took place, Jaben was fourteen. We changed the locks again (but only because we were redecorating) when Jaben was twenty-nine. He still had that same house key we'd given him at Christmas fifteen years before.

Chapter 6

Special Education Procedures, Technicalities, and Minutia

There are two kinds of teachers: those who know about special education and those who should. Virtually all teachers will participate in the instruction of disabled students and it behooves parents and educators to know both the limitations and expectations of special education law and procedure.

— DAVE FUNK

A Word of Warning

EVEN THOUGH I AM THOROUGHLY INVOLVED IN SPECIAL EDUCATION, actually read case law, and study procedure for recreation, there are aspects of the field that cause me to go into somewhat of an intellectual coma. My eyes glaze over, my brain shuts down, and I wonder if I understand anything at all. However, there are some things we need to know that we can't categorize as delightful and fun.

The reality is that all teachers, to one degree or another, are involved with disabled students and would do well to understand how to maneuver through special education without crashing. Thus the focus of this last chapter and a fair warning to the reader.

How Did Special Education Get Here?

Federal special education law is ultimately based on several diverse powers given to Congress by the Constitution. This includes the authority found in the interstate commerce clause (regulating activities between states) and the spending powers that allow Congress to condition the receipt of federal funds. In addition, special education law is based on the equal protection and due process clauses of the Fourteenth Amendment, as well as on civil rights legislation that addresses human dignity and self-worth. So the basis for special education has a foundation that goes to the heart of constitutional and human rights.

Laws that currently govern special education actually had their genesis in statutes created two hundred years ago. The first of these laws was passed by the Fifth Congress and addressed medical needs of sick and disabled sailors. Until the 1960s, the few other laws addressing disabilities were focused on the needs of war veterans with service-connected disabilities.

Since the 1960s, there has been an acceleration of federal legislation, state law, and court cases specifically related to racial discrimination, which in turn eventually affected laws related to the education of disabled students. In the case *Brown v. Board of Education*, a notable quote from the losing argument inadvertently associates the disabled with a number of other marginalized groups:

If the appellants' construction of the Fourteenth Amendment should prevail here, there is no doubt in my mind that it would catch the Indian within its grasp just as much as the Negro. If it should prevail, I am unable to see why a state would have any further right to segregate its pupils on the ground of sex or on the ground of age or on the ground of mental capacity.

Evidently, for some, disregarding certain groups as having little innate worth or value elicited no sense of moral conflict. Although about twenty years would pass before disabled students would receive benefit from this pivotal case, the Supreme Court's response was nevertheless encouraging. In the words of Judge Felix Frankfurter:

> Attitudes in this world are not changed abstractly, as it were, by reading something. . . . Attitudes are partly the result of working, attitudes are partly the result of action. . . . You do not fold your hands and wait for attitude to change by itself.

Here are some brief descriptions of the laws that specifically address the education of disabled students:

Rehabilitation Act of 1973: This law is critical because it prohibits discrimination against persons with disabilities and has a number of sections that deal with discrimination in employment (Section 501) as well as architectural and transportation barriers (Section 502). The component that would eventually most affect education is Section 504, which deals with nondiscrimination in programs or activities that receive federal aid. This condition was applied to public education in 1992, since which time schools have had to provide for students who are eligible for services under "Section 504."

Section 504 provides qualified disabled individuals with basic civil rights protection and prohibits otherwise qualified disabled individuals from being "excluded from the participation in, . . . denied the benefits of, or . . . subjected to discrimination under any program or activity receiving federal financial assistance."

Education for All Handicapped Children Act of 1975: This law, which grew out of a number of court cases and similar state laws, went into effect in 1977. It is the most influential law affecting special education and sets the fundamental provisions that have influenced subsequent court decisions and amendments. These provisions included free, appropriate, public education (FAPE) and due process protection for disabled children and their parents. This law also provides for an individualized education plan (IEP) that identifies the services necessary to ensure that a student's rights are observed.

This law has been amended a number of times. In 1983 (P.L. 98-199), Congress expanded incentives for preschool special education programs and placed responsibility for these laws with the Office of Special Education Programs (OSEP). In 1986 (P.L. 99-457), Congress mandated that schools be responsible for serving students starting at age three. In addition, birth-to-three programs were established (but were not the responsibility of the public school systems). In 1990 (P.L. 101-476), Congress passed an amendment to become known as the Individuals with Disabilities Education Act (IDEA).

Family Rights and Privacy Act (FERPA) of 1974: Also referred to as the Buckley Amendment, this law defines "educational records" and gives parents and students (the latter at the age of majority) the right to review personally identifiable information and request amendments if they believe documents contain inaccurate or misleading information. This act also addresses confidentiality issues for personally identifiable information.

Vocational Education Act of 1984: Often referred to as the Carl D. Perkins Act, this law authorizes federal funds to support vocational education programs. It provides for individuals who are members of special populations (including those with disabilities) to be given equal access to recruitment, enrollment, and placement in the full range of vocational education programs available to others.

Handicapped Children's Protection Act of 1986: This law authorizes the award of reasonable attorney fees to parents who prevail in due process or court hearings when there is a dispute with a school system relative to provisions of FAPE.

Temporary Child Care for Handicapped Children and Crisis Nurseries Act of 1986: This law provides funding to develop nonmedical respite and other family support services.

Developmental Disabilities and Bill of Rights Act of 1987: This act, together with subsequent amendments, provides grants to support university-affiliated programs and projects designed to increase independence, productivity, and integration of persons with disabilities.

Technology-Related Assistance for Individuals with Disabilities Act of 1988: The primary purpose of this act is to assist states in developing consumer-related programs and increase the availability of assistive technology to individuals with disabilities and their families.

Americans with Disabilities Act of 1990: The central purpose of this act is to extend civil rights protections to persons with disabilities commensurate with the rights afforded to others on the basis of race, sex, national origin, and religion.

Individuals with Disabilities Education Act (IDEA): This law emanated from the Education for All Handicapped Children Act of 1975 and has undergone a number of subsequent revisions (1990, 1997, 2004), each of which has fine-tuned previous versions. The 2004 revision involves a conscious effort to align with the No Child Left Behind (NCLB) Act, including the mandate that all teachers must meet the "highly qualified" standard.

No Child Left Behind (NCLB) Act of 2001: Although this law is not specifically special education legislation, it has an almost universal effect on our nation's schools. Because of its emphasis on schools' accountability for the achievement of all students, including the disabled, this law represents an initiative toward the federalization of education.

Note: Information about relevant laws is current as of the publication of this book. Since laws are periodically amended, the reader is encouraged to research updates of relevant legislation. In addition, the reader is reminded that descriptions in this book are for the purpose of identifying a generalized and global overview of relevant federal legislation. I am also fully aware that schools are subject to state laws that, although they are not to conflict with federal legislation, may involve specific definitions, procedural requirements, and other conditions. To understand the full requirements and provisions of these laws requires significant study of the actual statutes, subsequent regulations, and information provided by professionals competent in the area of special education legislation.

What Is the Comparative Status of Section 504 and IDEA?

ALTHOUGH SECTION 504 OF THE REHABILITATION ACT OF 1973 differs from the Individuals with Disabilities Education Act (IDEA) in areas such as specific definitions (e.g., "disability") and funding (Section 504 is not funded by federal dollars), both carry the full authority of federal law. Eligibility under Section 504 requires that a student (1) have a mental or physical impairment that (2) causes a disruption of a major life activity that (3) prevents access to opportunities that (4) they would otherwise be qualified for. Eligibility under IDEA requires that the student (1) have one or more of a given set of impairments that (2) cause adverse educational performance and (3) require specialized services (e.g., individualized instruction) as a result. IDEA procedural requirements are often considered more stringent; however, both laws provide a number of rights to parents, appropriate evaluation procedures, and provisions based on disability-related needs. In addition, IDEA carries a transition requirement whereas Section 504 does not.

What Is the Importance of Free, Appropriate, Public Education (FAPE)?

FAPE (RHYMES WITH TAPE) IS THE ACRONYM THAT DESCRIBES the special education "bottom line" for schools. Regardless of what special education law is being referenced, the essential meanings of the individual elements of this acronym are as follows:

Free: "Free" is fairly understandable and carries the sense that parents are to incur no additional cost for the child's special education services. This provision includes both direct costs (e.g., additional fees for instruction) and indirect costs (e.g., insurance deductibles or charges toward lifetime caps).

Appropriate: "Appropriate" is what makes special education special and verifies that a program will be designed based on the specified needs of an eligible student. Unless state law or district procedure so requires, "appropriate" is not understood as "best possible," nor as allowing the student to meet some identified maximum potential, nor even as allowing the student to attain other standards, such as skills, commensurate with other students of the same age/grade level. Rather, the requirement is for the student to make educational progress, gain access to school-related opportunity, and avoid being discriminated against on the basis of their handicapping condition.

Public: "Public" may well carry the most common connotation and indicates that, unless the child is under some other jurisdiction, the public school district in which the student resides is responsible for ensuring that all necessary educational services are provided. Neither parents nor outside agencies can be obligated to provide services or resources needed to meet the student's special education needs.

Education: The term "education" may need reorientation for some, because it involves more than academics. In addition to "reading, writing, and arithmetic," education also includes acquisition of intra- and interpersonal skills deemed important in our culture. Theoretically, unless an impairment inherently involves academic deficits (e.g., learning disabilities), a student could ostensibly have straight As and still have an educational disability. To avoid awkward pitfalls, the term "education" needs to be fully understood from a legal perspective as translated into educational language.

What Is a Legal Understanding of "Education"?

Simplistically, the student's role in education is to acquire knowledge and demonstrate skill mastery. A common understanding is that education involves only the development of academic skills and acquisition of content. However, within a more expanded definition, education includes academic, emotional, social, physical, health, communication, and vocational competencies. In addition to these discrete areas, there is a more subtle issue that evaluation teams have to deal with, encompassed by the term "general curriculum."

Perhaps more than any other factor, legislation has influenced the understanding of education in terms of proficiency, and proficiency is largely defined by test scores. In actuality, student learning has always been the emphasis, as evidenced in wording of the Education for All Handicapped Children Act of 1975 (and each subsequent law), and as reflected in the comments of the Supreme Court in *Board of Education of the Hendrick Hudson School District v. Rowley*, 458 U.S. 176 (1982), a precedent-setting case:

> When the language of the Act and its legislative history are considered together, the requirements imposed by Congress become tolerably clear. Insofar as a State is required to provide a handicapped child with a "free appropriate public education," we hold that it satisfies this requirement by providing personalized instruction with sufficient support services to permit the child to benefit educationally from that instruction.

Such instruction and services must be provided at public expense, must meet the State's educational standards, must approximate the grade levels used in the State's regular education, and must comport with the child's IEP. In addition, the IEP, and therefore the personalized instruction, should be formulated in accordance with the requirements of the Act and, if the child is educated in the regular classrooms of the public education system, should be reasonably calculated to enable the child to achieve passing marks and advance from grade to grade.

When the No Child Left Behind Act was initiated, a cry went out from many in special education that the laws were making them change yet again. The honest fact, however, is that the target has remained essentially the same, and that when education's aim gets far enough "off" to miss the mark, legislation is readied to force corrections.

Where Does "Special Education" Fit in the Realm of Instructional Adaptations?

THE TERM "SPECIAL EDUCATION" has come to represent a number of separate concepts. Sometimes it is used to differentiate from regular/general education. Sometimes it is used to identify a specific program, service, or even a room. However, the term primarily refers to instruction that is designed in accordance with a student's disability-related characteristics. As it were, special education is instruction that is specifically constructed (i.e., "designed") to meet the unique (educational) needs of the student resulting from the disability. This instruction is based on the characteristics of the child's disability, determined through evaluation, that cause adverse educational performance. Without such analysis, there is a tendency to form an overdependence on teacher preference, conformity to an educational methodology, or constraints of district curricula.

There are basically five levels of instructional adaptation within any educational system:

1. *Choice and variety:* The first level simply constitutes the choice and variety that are part of normal, good teaching. These adaptations are often made on the basis of keeping the class motivated or interested rather than on the basis of any specific individual need, and do not alter a normal grading system that reflects only the student's demonstration of skill mastery.

2. *Grade differentiation:* A second level is grade differentiation. To be consistent with judicious principles, grades should reflect proficiency, so a student receiving an A in a particular subject should have an objectively higher skill level than someone receiving a C. Essentially, traditional letter grades should be determined by tasks of skill mastery (e.g., test scores) rather than by tasks designed for practice or skill acquisition (e.g., homework).

3. *Accommodations:* The third level is the starting point for making adaptations on the basis of needs of a protected class of students based on formal evaluation. "Accommodations" involve adaptations that are made for individual students who meet some eligibility criteria for some type of protection (e.g., "handicapped" under Section 504, "limited English proficient," or "IDEA eligible"). Accommodations do not alter the regular education content or proficiency expectations. Preferential seating, providing additional time to finish tests, and allowing a student to demonstrate content knowledge via a verbal presentation rather than a written report would all be examples. Like choice and variety, as indicated above, accommodations should not require any departure from the regular grading system.

4. *Modifications:* "Modifications" are a fourth level of adaptation. Like accommodations, modifications are made on an individual basis for students meeting eligibility for a protected class of persons. However, in contrast to accommodations, modifications are

adaptations that alter either or both the content and the proficiency expectations of the regular education content. Examples may range from reducing a spelling list to making significant changes in a test. At the modification level, the normal curricular requirements are altered and may have ramifications for grading or even the type of graduation document granted. By definition, modifications indicate that the normal grade or age skill levels have not been attained.

5. *Special education:* The adaptations discussed thus far are understood to be relative to the curriculum that is applicable to the disabled student's nondisabled peers. Special education, the fifth level of adaptation, involves alterations in content, methodology, or delivery of instruction that go beyond the normal purview of regular education and fundamentally alter the content and proficiency expectations when compared to the achievement of nondisabled students. Designing instruction on the basis of individual disability-related variables requires teachers who do not allow their efforts to be limited by their previous training, curricular philosophy, availability of materials, or teaching-style preferences.

Who Is on the "Team" and What Do They Do?

THERE IS NO INDICATION THAT THE COMPOSITION of the evaluation team substantially changes from the time a kid is referred to the very end of the process. A full complement of professional opinion is expected when making determinations of eligibility, programming, and placement. Appointments to the team include persons who have familiarity with the legal process, understanding of disabilities and related issues, knowledge about the child, ability to determine appropriate instruction, and authority to commit district resources.

Parents (and students when appropriate) are to be involved throughout the process, and they generally have the prerogative of bringing whomever they wish to any formal meeting. In contrast, the school is responsible for ensuring that given positions are represented.

What Evaluation Positions Should Be Represented by the School?

Contingent upon district practice, one person on the evaluation team can perform more than one function, if he or she is properly qualified and a mutually exclusive circumstance is not created. Although individual state laws and local district policies will have specific requirements, there are four positions that should always be represented by the school when eligibility, programming, service, or placement decisions are made:

1. *A district representative authorized to allocate resources and ensure procedural correctness.* Referred to as the local education agency (LEA) representative, this person is someone authorized by the school district to commit resources sufficient to fulfill the obligations of the evaluation team's decisions. This requires that the LEA representative have a working knowledge of resources throughout the district. Often, this position is filled by an administrator who has thorough knowledge of resources only at a building level.

    Another primary role of this person is to ensure that both the documents and the process are procedurally and substantively correct. Because of this responsibility, the person carries authority to require the obtainment of information that is sufficient to substantiate any consideration. Another function that often falls to this person is determining what action will be taken if school staff cannot come to consensus. This decision-making authority requires high-level knowledge of special education principles. (Note: In the case that consensus is not obtained between the parents and the school, the parents generally have a right to appeal.)

2. *A teacher or provider knowledgeable about special education issues relevant to the student being evaluated.* The person in this position is required to be appropriately qualified (e.g., certified) and is responsible for providing information about disability-based performance, appropriate instruction, required services, and resources necessary to implement the evaluation team's decisions. Unless there are extenuating circumstances, this person is, has been, or is anticipated to be the student's special education instructor.

3. *A person knowledgeable about the student from an educational perspective.* Because this person must be knowledgeable about the student's regular education performance, he or she is virtually always the student's regular education teacher. Because there are so few exceptions, when special education services that involve the general curriculum or placement are being considered, a regular education teacher should always participate. If the student has a number of teachers, not all necessarily have to attend evaluation meetings unless there are extenuating circumstances. However, all regular education teachers should be aware of their responsibilities in the implementation of any plan developed.

    Regular education teachers are recognized as having a high level of professional skill and are expected to contribute significantly to the issues of program modification, support for school personnel, resource allocations necessary for the student to succeed in the regular education environment, and even the development of behavioral interventions.

4. *A person qualified to interpret educational assessment information.* Evaluation teams are expected to be accountable for making decisions on the basis of objective information. Although the person fulfilling this position does not necessarily need credentials to administer particular tests or perform other procedures (e.g., a psychological evaluation), a level of training and experience sufficient to accurately discuss the instructional ramifications of such information is presumed.

It is to be emphasized that the positions mentioned above are the basics. However, the particular circumstances may require additional representation. For instance, in the state of Wisconsin, there are potentially eleven such positions with different scenarios (e.g., representatives from private schools, resident districts under "open enrollment," transition service providers, etc.).

What Is Needed for a Kid to Be Determined Educationally Disabled?

A PRIMARY PURPOSE OF EVALUATION is to determine if a student is eligible for services beyond what can be provided within regular education. This decision requires more than simply reading a few test scores and comparing the data with some predetermined formula. Making conclusions with such limited information is shortsighted and establishes the misconception that simply having an identifiable condition is sufficient to qualify a student for special education services. Such is absolutely not the case.

Being disabled means much more than having some trouble in school. Although specific eligibility criteria are determined by individual states and there are some differences between IDEA and Section 504, there are three components that need to be established to declare any student as truly educationally handicapped:

1. *Impairment:* Impairments are slippery little characters, because the same term can have different meanings within the educational, psychological, and medical communities. Some noneducational professionals falsely presume they have the prerogative to make pronouncements for other domains. As handy as it may be for a medical doctor to write "has ADD and needs special education" on a prescription pad, such is not binding on a school district. Unless there is some legal involvement (e.g., due process hearing), the

agency providing FAPE makes all final decisions (with parents having appeal rights if they do not agree).

Impairments are conditions that conform to given descriptors. Under IDEA, these conditions are identified in federal law and further delineated by individual states. Under Section 504, a more global terminology of "mental or physical impairment causing a disruption of a major life activity" is used. Evaluation teams should always have the actual law, state education department–approved worksheets, or other guides for reference as they make these decisions. Special education is far too complicated to rely only on memory. It is remarkable how many students are enrolled in special needs programs who do not actually qualify because specific regulations, written for the very purpose of avoiding inappropriate determinations, were not consulted.

2. *Adverse educational performance:* This is the hidden factor in the determination of eligibility. Although the wording of many conditions includes "that results in adverse educational performance," this is often not directly addressed by evaluation teams. Overlooking this single factor violates the causal mandate. Any number of kids have impairments and performance deficits. What takes expertise is determining a causal relationship. Also, "adverse" indicates serious problems. If such soft phrases as "has difficulty" or "struggles with" accurately describes a kid's performance, the intended standard of deficit has likely not been met. Special education's penchant for euphemisms needs to be stopped. Trying to make people feel good about a bad situation is not all that noble.

3. *Need for specialized intervention:* The term "special education" is variously used to differentiate from regular education, refer to a place (e.g., resource classroom), identify an impairment stereotype (e.g., learning disabilities instruction), or sometimes even equate to a particular methodology (e.g., Orton Gillingham). The point in determining if a student has a disability is that the student's

impairment-related educational needs cannot be addressed even with significant adaptations within the regular classroom environment. Special education is customized instruction to address the unique disability-related characteristics of the student that are causing adverse educational performance. This instruction is designed for the student and goes well beyond helping with homework, assisting in class, or supervising behavior.

What Is Assessment Supposed to Find Out?

Evaluation teams are commissioned to gather information sufficient to document "comparative status" between the student and peer group, "causal relationship" between the condition and any identified adverse educational performance, and "characteristics" of the disability:

1. *Comparative status:* To a large degree, being handicapped is relative to what is considered the norm on a national basis. Being identified as a poor reader or of low intelligence is based on a student's ranking in a comparison group. Although measuring students this way may fluctuate, have exceptions to the rule, and be replete with other faults, the use of standardized tests is probably the lesser evil, considering the options. Because many impairment conditions are defined by standardized information, to disregard an objective score requires substantial justification.

    However, if evaluation teams simply look at scores without a proper understanding of the process, inaccuracies will often be introduced from the very beginning of the process, and have a multiplier effect throughout. Too many students are declared eligible for special education services essentially on the basis of a score that tells little more than where they are standing in line compared with their peers. And truth be told, anyone who is familiar with the kid usually knows this pretty much already. If the assessment process stops here, the basis for misdiagnosis has been solidly set.

2. ***Causal relationship:*** Identifying whether a student has some condition (e.g., ADD, low IQ, reading deficit, etc.) is a relatively simple act of comparing scores with predetermined criteria that requires little skill or insight. Within special education, it is insufficient that two phenomena simply coexist (e.g., emotional deficits and behavior problems). Lots of things correlate, and I suspect a great many superstitions exist because two events happened in closed proximity.

   Determining if there is a causal relationship requires high-level professional expertise and skill. Giving a test is relatively easy. Acceptable responses are usually on the protocol, and scoring is often computerized. What takes high-level thinking is deciding what information is needed and how to analyze the data gathered. This emphasizes why a number of procedures are necessary. Tests may give some very valuable information, but their value is accentuated when coupled with data from other sources. The answer to the question of causality must be "yes" or "no." There is no provision for "maybe." If the evaluation team cannot decide, there are few options but to obtain more information.

3. ***Characteristics:*** A third piece of information derived from assessment is determining the characteristics of the condition manifested by the individual student. This is perhaps where the highest professional skill is required, because the evaluation team must separate disability-related issues from the student's temperament, value base, and other nondisability factors that influence educational performance. Identifying the characteristics manifested by the disability becomes the foundation for identifying goals, developing instruction, and assessing performance. In addition, this is a critical piece of information for students facing disciplinary actions such as placement changes and expulsions.

About Tests

Within special education, evaluation is to involve a variety of procedures. As a result, administering formal testing, regardless of how many instruments may be administered, is considered one procedure. Therefore, documented observation, interviews, parental surveys, and other assessment procedures are to be given appropriate consideration and status. This requirement emphasizes the need for a number of perspectives to fully understand the child.

Tests can certainly provide details for purposes of eligibility and programming. When standardized scores are required, formal tests are virtually the only source of such information. However, those giving a test must be able to do much more than record a student's response, determine a raw score, and check a chart for age or grade equivalents. Tests are hardly real-life, and the results have to be analyzed and correlated with other aspects of the student's performance.

Another caution in assessment is the practice of test playing, which can be a rather sophisticated game. Giving only parts of a test and representing the results as a global indication of a student's skill, altering the standard response format, or cueing the student to "see what they really know" should not be done, despite being easy to rationalize. Doing so simply undermines the process, let alone the credibility of those who engage in such practices.

The Importance of Determining the Unique Special Education Need

Although the student's unique special education need is the essential element driving special education, it is often not given due consideration. Instead, the focus is more often on the visible manifestations (e.g., academic or behavioral deficits that can be observed) extrapolated from the impairment condition.

Regardless, the instructional plan developed is to provide services to address the student's "unique special education need," described as follows:

1. ***The need must directly result from the student's impairment.*** This determination requires appropriate evaluation and analysis of behavior, learning patterns, and characteristics that interfere with educational performance. These determinations are important not only for the immediate instructional planning that needs to be done, but also for future eventualities (e.g., disciplinary removals that engage procedural safeguards such as a manifestation determination).

2. ***The need must be a salient factor in the student's lack of success in the educational setting.*** This may include emotional/behavioral, learning, social, or physical issues. For instance, a speech/language student who is refusing to hand in assignments to irritate a teacher probably doesn't count as being a disability-related concern. Essentially, if a characteristic doesn't cause a problem, it isn't a need.

3. ***The need must be consistent with the characteristics of the impairment condition.*** Frankly, this third part of the definition is stated with some trepidation, because there may be a tendency for evaluation teams to make conclusions based on a group stereotype rather than based on the student as an individual. However, impairment conditions are defined, and to disregard these definitions gives rise to error in diagnoses, interventions, and services.

Unique Need or Manifestation?

There is also often a confusion between the unique need and the manifestation of the impairment. Unless there is a distinct differentiation between these two concepts, it is a relatively simple task to conclude that just about any maladaptive behavior can be attributed to just about any impairment condition.

I once read a case about a language-impaired student who was caught passing drugs and subsequently expelled. He was eventually exonerated because a court determined that his illegal action was related to his impairment. The tactic the court used is similar to a word puzzle in which you start with one word, substitute a letter with each step, and end up with a completely different word by making just one small change at a time.

The justification made on behalf of this student was that, first of all, he had limited language ability and was shunned by other students. The court reasoned that this contributed to a negative self-concept and that, in order for this student to gain a feeling of acceptance, he became a willing dupe for his more sophisticated peers. Voilà, selling drugs was a result of his language impairment! Given this premise, there are few instances in which a relationship between two isolated conditions could *not* be shown.

As described above, a unique special education need has a direct causal relationship to the student's impairment. Certainly, individual characteristics must be considered, and it is acknowledged that a student's experience, temperament, and other factors certainly influence perception. However, unless the source of the problem is addressed and not just the symptoms, the drift effect in special education will continue unabated.

Who Decides How and What the Kid Is Taught?

EVALUATION TEAMS ARE OFTEN PRESSURED to provide a specific methodology as part of a student's special education. First, teams must remember that the agency providing FAPE has "first dibs" on deciding what instructional strategies are to be implemented. If these strategies are demonstrated as effective, even the courts will likely defer to the schools. But in spite of this, heated arguments still often arise.

Problems of methodology occur when decisions are made on the basis of preference (parent or staff), lack of knowledge about differentiating and individualizing instruction, or any other reason that is not directly related to the student's disability. Of prime consideration is the idea that adopting a specific methodology, without modification, may well violate the mandate to individualize. After all, in hardly any case has a specific methodology been developed for an individual kid in the first place.

However difficult the discussion of methodology may be, identifying the salient characteristics that designate instruction as "specially designed" clarifies the intervention intended by the evaluation team. In addition, identifying characteristics of the instruction conveys a sense of confidence that the anticipated plan meets that standard of appropriateness.

Historically, in response to the development of special education categories, certification areas arose to address the presumed and anticipated needs for professional development. As a result, special education became segmented and specialized. In far too many instances, regular education was effectively removed from the process of differentiating instruction and accommodating for diverse learners. This became a philosophical basis for teachers declining to involve themselves with kids' behavior, toileting, or anything else they didn't want to do.

In 1992, when schools were mandated to provide services under Section 504, many regular education teachers rightly believed they were ill prepared to develop modifications for handicapped students. The initiatives of the 1997 IDEA amendments adopted the stance that regular education teachers brought an expertise sufficient to be equal partners with special education in addressing the instruction *and* behavior of disabled students. No longer were there specialists with secret knowledge who could unilaterally determine eligibility and programming. The law required a recognition that appropriate instruction involves input from a number of perspectives on a "different role, equal status" basis.

Appropriate instruction and services are to be based on information constituting (1) a description of the student's current performance, and (2) the goals to be accomplished.

Description of Current Performance

In a sense, this section of the written plan is the student's special education résumé and serves as the transition between what is known about the student (from experience and evaluation) and what will be done in response to the identified needs. Information contained in this section can be somewhat varied, but should include the following details about the student:

1. *Specific skill levels:* Since information in this section serves as the basis for subsequent determination of goals/objectives, services, and placement, wording should precisely reflect the student. "Feel good" euphemisms, overgeneralized terms, or ambiguous comments are not appropriate and can actually deter the evaluation team from making accurate decisions. Additionally, the information should be presented in a usable form. It should be kept in mind that normed-referenced scores from standardized instruments usually lack information relevant to instructional programming. Such reporting essentially identifies a student's raw score; however, the same raw score can represent very different profiles. Even if there is a thorough analysis of individual responses, there is limited instructional value. For purposes of instruction, proficiency levels are best determined from criterion-referenced instruments, documented observation, work samples, and other real-life measures.

2. *Learning characteristics of the student:* This information should include how the impairment affects the student's ability to acquire skills and knowledge. In turn, this information should be related to the student's degree of involvement in the normal educational

environment. This is more than determining a "learning style" and involves both the intellectual and the affective aspects of the student. By identifying the student's learning characteristics, instructional teams have a foundation for determining effective methodology and supports that might be required.

3. *Response to previous interventions:* How a student has responded to previous interventions is of importance in determining what future strategies and techniques would be appropriate. In special education there is a tendency to utilize and refine strategies that are comfortable to the teacher—regardless of their effect on the student. Also, the chance that interventions developed in isolation will have spectacular successes is slim. To know what has (or has not) worked for a particular student in the past is a much firmer foundation for making decisions. Given the expenditure of time, effort, and resources devoted to special education, efficiency is not an altogether bad thing.

Going from Where the Kid Is to Where We Want the Kid to Be

An IEP goal that was brought to my attention some years ago read, "The long-term and short-term goals are the same, the only difference being the degree to which each is accomplished." I was never confident I knew what that meant.

For goals to give direction to the instructional team and fulfill their intended purpose, the following information needs to be embedded within them:

1. *Unique special education need:* The unique special education need of the student identifies what directly results from the disability that causes the educational concern. Without this determination, goals will simply concentrate on a manifestation (academic, social, emotional, etc.), with little indication of what the specially

designed instruction should really be addressing. For instance, the student's disability may cause a limitation in abstraction (the unique need), which may in turn affect reading comprehension (the manifestation), which may in turn affect involvement in the general curriculum.

2. ***Attainment at a sufficient level to develop foundational skills:*** Although there is no single level that would be universally appropriate, whatever would provide a foundation for subsequent learning is a commonsense standard. This, actually, is a rather high number (e.g., ninety percent) in most cases. For comparison, think of the expected level of mastery in the real world: What percentage of inaccuracy would be acceptable in language to avoid confusion? How accurate do people want their payroll workers to be? And the list could go on and on. The point is to determine a level of attainment that is sufficient for long-term learning.

   I once read a goal that stated the student would engage in a particular behavior at a ten percent level. When asked the justification for this low number, the answer was that he didn't engage in the behavior at all at the time the IEP was written. The truth of the matter was that the behavior being discussed was not appropriate as an instructional goal. I have also seen goals set ridiculously high, supposedly as an encouragement. To whom, I don't know—certainly not the kid. To state a goal to be accomplished at a sufficient level, the evaluation team may have to narrow its focus. The old adage of "biting off more than one can chew" is especially appropriate to remember. Without this parameter, we may have the special education equivalent of "a jack of all trades and master of none."

3. ***Involvement and progress in general curriculum:*** The student's access to the general curriculum (under Section 504) or progress in it (under IDEA) must be addressed. In addition, other educational needs (i.e., academic, emotional, social, communication, vocational, physical, and health) are to be addressed, provided these needs are a direct result of the disability.

4. *Specification of the instructional domain:* I once read a goal that stated, "[Student] will increase his knowledge base." Although I am all for everyone increasing their knowledge base, in the case of this student, I had no idea about what that would involve. Even reading the component objectives gave no further clues (one was about the student increasing completion of homework—again, a fine thing to articulate, but it shed very little light on what was to be done). The reader of a goal should be able to ascertain whether the instruction will be in an academic, emotional, social, or other realm.

5. *Identification of a measurable attainment level:* For most teachers, this is often the hardest part of writing a goal. To overcome this problem, many have adopted a "standard response." I have read any number of goals that indicate an age or grade equivalent increase (one year's worth being the most popular) or a given percentage of accuracy (eighty percent seems to be the all-time favorite). "Measurable" conveys the understanding that a student's performance is quantifiable. This is especially relevant given the fact that (under IDEA), evaluation teams are mandated to periodically report the student's progress toward the goal.

    Eventually, the question of "Did the student arrive?" (i.e., accomplish the goal) has to be answered "yes" or "no." There needs to be a tangibly identifiable end result. If I were to ask whether an airplane listed as going to Denver would really end up there, a "maybe," "we don't know," or even "we think so" would not be very comforting. Similar answers concerning whether a goal has been met are equally disconcerting, and certainly are not adequate to meet the expected standard.

Whenever I am formally instructing a class in IEP development, a cry goes out for an example. I have learned to hesitate, not because having a model is inappropriate, but because the model often becomes a rigid formula. Goals are just as individualized as any other part of the written document. So, with my eyes wide open, I offer the following example with an ambiguous "Chris" as the student:

Utilizing replacement behaviors taught as part of an anger management program, Chris will increase self-discipline skills as demonstrated by reducing violations of the Code of Conduct that result in removal from class from an average of three per week to no more than two per month.

Does this illustration contain all five of the elements listed above? I certainly realize that "decrease discipline problems" would be a whole lot easier to write, but this would not have much more value than stating, "Chris will be less annoying to adults."

How Is It Decided Whether the Kid Gets "Extra" Services?

THERE IS OFTEN SIGNIFICANT CONFUSION in differentiating special education (e.g., designed instruction) from the other services associated with special education. It is critical, however, to make this determination. Unless students qualify for special education, they are not eligible for the other provisions of supplementary and related aids and services. To avoid misapplication of these provisions, the evaluation team should have a working knowledge of what these services entail:

1. *Related services:* Related services are provisions necessary for the student to benefit from their special education. Essentially, these services act as catalysts necessary for the special education to work. Therefore, a discussion of such services (e.g., occupational therapy, speech/language services, counseling, etc.) must be held in abeyance until the specially designed instruction is determined. Then the evaluation team must justify why, for lack of the specific related service, the special education would be ineffective. It is not just a matter of whether the student "could use" the related service; rather it is a matter of its necessity relative to implementing the specially designed instruction.

There is provision in IDEA that if a student requires only a related service, and that if this related service is very like special education, the student can qualify as disabled. This is a great reminder that special education law is not exempt from cyclical reasoning.

2. *Supplementary aids and services:* Supplementary aids and services are adaptations made for individual students, generally relative to their participation in a regular education environment. If a student needs only this level of adaptation, to be labeled "disabled" is a misnomer. Supplementary aids and services are roughly commensurate with accommodations and have as their primary purpose to maintain a disabled student's participation in a regular education environment to the degree appropriate. These provisions "level the playing field," so to speak, by offsetting the limitations of the disability. However, their purpose is not to give the disabled student any unfair advantage or alter the essential qualities of a program. Although some may view these supports as a mandate to have a student placed in a regular classroom at all costs, such is not the case. The benefit to the student and any relative harmful effect to others are always considerations.

    This is one place in the process that input from the regular education teacher has preeminence. Since regular education teachers are the most qualified source of information about the regular education classroom, their opinion about what the student needs in order to be successful in that environment should be given considerable deference.

3. *Program modifications:* Whereas supplementary aids and services do not alter the essential qualities of a course of study, program modifications can make significant changes for the individual student. This provision authorizes the team to make any alterations necessary to address the student's disability-related needs. This may include a different curriculum, adapted grading, provisions for behavior management, or any other adaptation that alters the fundamental components of the way things are normally done.

Although the evaluation team has authority (within procedural guidelines) to make these adaptations, modifications may certainly have significant ramifications. For instance, changes that affect curriculum content or proficiency expectations would result in some type of adapted grading system. This may significantly affect the granting of a regular high school diploma, may affect overall grade point average and class rank, and may restrict options available for vocational/career training. Modifications to the regular program must be considered and implemented if appropriate, but they potentially carry serious long-term consequences.

4. *Personnel supports:* This is the one place in the written document that focuses on the service providers. Those who framed the special education legislation realized that because special education students, by definition, have unique and significant needs, up-to-date training is necessary. Just as in other professions that are not static, teachers and other service providers are expected to keep abreast of current information in their fields. Of course, this does not justify being swayed by every methodological breeze, but new information (e.g., brain research) is constantly being made available that can greatly assist in making instructional decisions.

There is too often a push for students to receive all sorts of supportive services. However, the key is whether the student requires these services to access their education without violating the broader goals of special education (e.g., independence and employability).

How Is It Decided Where the Kid Goes to School?

Although "placement" ostensibly concerns where the student's body will be, there are a number of considerations that go into this decision.

Sometimes this final portion of the process is easy, because few adjustments on the student's part may be needed. The student will remain in the same school, have the same regular education teacher(s), and have to deal with only minor adjustments in their schedule.

Sometimes, however, placement determinations become unbelievably confrontational, conflicted, and difficult to make. These complications often arise when the evaluation team is considering alternative placements outside the student's attendance-area school. Where a student is educated often carries significant emotional ramifications.

When Location Is an Issue (Nondisciplinary)

There are any number of legitimate reasons why an appropriate education may not be providable at the student's attendance-area school. Accessibility is certainly one issue. If the student's disability limits mobility, a multistory school with no elevator may be deemed inappropriate. In a situation of low-incidence disability, there may be an economic factor to consider. That is, there may be insufficient numbers of students in a particular school to justify the necessary staffing. Even space considerations can be a factor. Students may be required to attend a particular school because appropriate programming is available only at a given location.

Another, albeit extreme, reason is referred to as "hostile environment." When a condition exists (generally between a school and parents or the student) that is so adversarial that there is no reasonable expectation the student will benefit from any services provided, another school is a legitimate solution. Such situations are fairly rare and should not necessarily be fostered, but in some cases the relationship between a particular school and parents is so toxic that an appropriate education for the student is prohibited.

What Is the Importance of Procedural and Substantive Correctness?

It is of extreme importance that both the special education process and the subsequent document produced be procedurally and substantively correct. In the event of any legal challenge, these aspects will be among the first scrutinized.

Procedural aspects involve the actual logistics—the rules, as it were. Adhering to timelines, completing forms appropriately, conforming to legal definitions, and properly implementing a student's individual plan are all parts of procedural correctness.

Attention to the substantive correctness of special education documentation (i.e., correctness of its actual content) is also crucial. In the early years of special education litigation, districts were usually faulted on the basis of procedural errors. The presumption was that since professionals were involved, the content must be appropriate. (Why the courts would think so seems more likely an indication that lawyers and judges didn't know what to do with disabled students either.) Increasingly, however, the appropriateness of the content of special education documentation has given emphasis. Therefore, wording, type and use of data, and internal consistency have gained significance.

What Information Is Needed When Programming for Behavior Change?

The following process is suggested as a means for evaluation teams to identify the function of a behavior:

1. *Identify the behavior in descriptive terms.* An operational definition is one that is free of subjectivity. That is, the description would be anticipated to be essentially and accurately understood even by those not directly involved. Too often, phrases like "has difficulty

with" are used to describe a wide range of behavior. Such imprecision is counterproductive.

The instructional team should determine if the precipitating behavior is part of a pattern. Certainly, there will be times when the behavior at issue will be isolated and uncharacteristic of the student—a one-time occurrence. However, since in most cases the student will have been removed for a substantial number of days already, there will be ample behavioral incidents to consider. Determining a pattern of behavior is important in identifying whether there is a causal relationship between the behavior and the disability. This is necessary not only in instances where manifestation determinations are involved, but also in determining attribution and subsequent development of intervention strategies.

2. *Identify the context of the behavior.* This involves analyzing the behavior in the element in which it occurs. Antecedents, overt reactions of the student and others, and the actual and anticipated results (consequences) of the behavior are all components of the behavioral context. (For instance, it may be observed that the student consistently gains attention after the behavior is elicited and comes to anticipate this form of validation of personhood.)

Known characteristics of the student as well as the disability are also part of the context. Although the basic principles of human behavior discussed above would continue to be valid, if the student's disability distorts reality, and if this reality is significantly different than that of the evaluators, there may be some truly unique twists to the team's conclusions and resultant placement/programming decisions. For instance, a student may refuse to comply with teacher directives because of a perception that his autonomy is being taken away if he does what others tell him to do. Regardless of the reasonableness of a teacher's order, the perceptual set, influenced by the (emotional) disability, distorts the reality of the situation.

3. *Identify where the behavior does not occur.* In nearly all cases concerning volitional behavior, there will be some environments and circumstances in which the behavior has not occurred nor is anticipated to occur. Understanding the characteristics of these circumstances and environments is a vital part of understanding the behavior itself.

4. *Translate the analysis into a paradigm.* The ultimate focus of behavior analysis is to determine the "payoff" to the student resulting from the behavior. Since this payoff has already been shown to effectively maintain the behavior, the replacement behavior (in the case of a behavior plan) should result in the same reinforcer. Perhaps this would be as simple as providing legitimate choices or as complicated as switching from control over others to self-control. The point is, the new behavior being taught must satisfy the same basic need that the maladaptive behavior did.

Generally, What Information Should Go Into a Behavior Plan?

SPECIAL EDUCATION IS REPLETE WITH FORMS, and another one is not really needed. Although such tools can make a process more efficient, it must be recognized that any strict form is developed based on variables that might not be consistent from situation to situation. With the goal of developing a tool that is more versatile, the suggested format below provides an outline for a behavior plan:

1. *Target behavior:* The first consideration is to specifically identify the behavior. Often, evaluation teams attach nebulous or subjective terms to behavior (e.g., "reduce disruptive behavior"). Whether the intent is to be tactful or avoid harshness, being nonspecific simply clouds the process and efficiency. When wording such as "has difficulty following rules" is used, little

usable information is conveyed. Rather, the behavior in question needs to be so specifically identified that even those unfamiliar with the student will have a precise understanding of the behavioral goal. Remember, plans are written not only for those who are involved in their development, but also for those who will be implementing and potentially reviewing the plan in the future. The point being, the language should be clear, even to those who have not directly participated in the development of the plan.

2. *Context of the behavior:* Although not all instances will require an extensive or formal assessment, the context in which the behavior is occurring is extremely important. Such factors as time, location, and what happens before and after the incident can be vital. In addition, where the behavior does not occur can also offer clues about its management. Additionally, the evaluation team also needs to ascertain fundamental functional factors such as what the student gains or avoids as a result of the behavior. This may often require observation or analysis from someone with "another perceptual box," because sometimes those most intimately involved with the behavior often have a field of awareness that prohibits objective analysis.

3. *Replacement behavior:* Establishing what the affective "payoff" is (i.e., determination of what is maintaining the target behavior) provides some parameters for identifying replacement behavior. To be effective, the replacement behavior should address the same need for the student as did the target behavior. The replacement behavior should not result in a violation of self-worth or autonomy, or sense of consequence.

4. *Interventions:* In instances of behavior management, characteristics of the intervention will be identified in the student's specially designed instruction. As such, this would be defined as adaptation of content and methodology, and delivery of instruction. Therefore, each applicable component should be clearly identified

in the behavior plan. For many students, this intervention will constitute their special education (i.e., specially designed instruction to address issues resulting from the impairment condition).

5. *Monitoring:* Whether monitoring is documented through charting, anecdotal records, or some other vehicle, a key to success is consistently following through on the plan. This monitoring should involve the student as more than a bystander watching the adults. Also integral is identifying who needs to know about the plan and what part they may have in its implementation.

6. *Evidence of student involvement:* Although it is important to physically involve the student, little will be accomplished if they perceive the process as not really including them, or if they are simply being manipulated by the process. If there is a team orientation of "different role, equal status," involvement of the student creates a balance that can reduce issues of conflict and counterproductive talk.

7. *Criteria for success/failure of the plan:* There should be built-in markers for determining the success or failure of any behavior plan. As part of this "schedule" of such markers, the instructional team can determine the rate of improvement, time-related benchmarks, and other indicators that will identify mutually agreeable signs regarding the student's progress.

8. *Environmental changes:* Another factor that should be considered from the initiation of the plan constitutes the environmental changes that will need to be made to implement it. To a large degree, a student's misbehavior is related in some way to the environment in which it occurs. If the IEP team identifies environmental variables or interaction dynamics that contribute to the student's misbehavior, there is a reasonable expectation for these aspects to be modified. This is not to exonerate the student for wrong conduct, but it seems unreasonable to expect only the student to change.

9. *Timeline:* Identifying a time context is also an important factor, to reduce the perception that permanent behavior changes happen immediately. The evaluation team should identify chronological markers that indicate when various phases of the plan can be expected to be accomplished.

When Should Special Needs Kids Be Taught the Same Thing and in the Same Place as Their Nondisabled Peers?

WHENEVER ESOTERIC CONCEPTS ARE INTRODUCED, operational definitions should be developed to preclude as much confusion as possible. Such is the case for three terms that are often erroneously interchanged:

Least restrictive environment (LRE): LRE was long ago defined as any location in which a majority of students are nondisabled. Although being taught alongside nondisabled students may presuppose being involved in the general curriculum, there is no such absolute necessity. To normalize the educational experience of disabled kids, discriminatory segregation on the basis of disability is to be avoided. The presupposition is that students should have access to and participate in regular education classrooms, as well as in extracurricular and other nonacademic activities, alongside their nondisabled peers.

Regular education: Whereas LRE is closely related to place, regular education is associated with what is being taught and the methodologies used. Regular education is often equated with grade-level curriculum and with similar-age peers. In addition, content and instructional strategies of "regular education" may well involve a rather significant continuum of adaptations without rising to the level of special education. Since the content contained in regular education is justified on the basis of societal as well as academic benefit, disabled students should not be isolated from such information without having their due process rights considered.

Although the validity of particular content, developmentally appropriate tasks, and other philosophical issues may generate extensive arguments, much more emphasis needs to be placed on appropriate involvement of the student within the overall district-approved curriculum. Progress in the general curriculum (as per IDEA) or access to it (as per Section 504) does not mean forced participation, exposure only, or keeping up with nondisabled peers. What it does mean is that the disabled student has opportunity to develop a knowledge base common to the normal educational experience.

Inclusion: To equate the general curriculum with a level of regular classroom involvement (e.g., "full" or "partial") would perpetuate an inadequate concept. The term "inclusion" does not appear in statutory law and has been developed to define an educational philosophy. In some ways, the term is artificial, and as is far too common in education, the philosophy can become so pervasive that the requirement to develop the disabled student's special education program based on individual needs is violated.

Inclusion is ultimately an LRE issue and means that the disabled student is not denied commensurate opportunity for access to normal educational experiences without due process protection. Additionally, the inclusion philosophy originally presumed the disabled student's education was the responsibility of both regular and special education. Without this joint ownership, placing a disabled student into a regular education environment is often viewed more as "intrusion" and violates the underlying rationale originally established by the originators of the concept.

A Final Word

THE INTENT OF THIS LAST CHAPTER has not been to address every concern that arises in special education, but to give some ideas about issues that commonly arise. Whenever procedural or legal questions occur, those within the educational system need to have a thorough working knowledge of district, state, and federal guidelines. This is not to imply that educators need to be legal experts. The wise person knows when their sphere of knowledge has been exhausted and other professionals need to be called in. Special education is so complicated that no one can stay in isolation and come out ahead. At some point, all students will be done with their schooling. As individual students approach this point in their lives, it becomes acutely apparent that we all need to work together in getting special needs kids ready for the real world.

Index

About the Author

DAVID FUNK WAS TEACHING KIDS with significant learning and behavioral problems well before the advent of special education law. This extensive perspective has provided him with an opportunity to identify what has long-term effectiveness with challenging kids. He first learned about Love and Logic in the early 1980s—almost "on accident," as kids would say—and decided he would try it out. Taking small steps, he experimented to see if the concepts taught by Jim Fay and Foster Cline really would work. They did, and David spent the next several years focusing on how to apply these concepts to special needs students in terms of their behavior and achievement. David has promoted Love and Logic through the development of graduate courses, workshops, and conference presentations to a wide range of audiences. His message and focus has always been the same: getting kids ready for the real world.

Over his nearly forty-year career as public school teacher, university faculty member, administrator, and presenter, David has been granted a number of awards in recognition of his contributions to education. He and his wife, Diane, reside in Brown Deer, Wisconsin, and have two adult married children—Aleshia, married to Dave, and Jaben, married to Jen—as well as a grandson, Edrik. In addition to writing *Getting Special Needs Kids Ready for the Real World*, David is author of *Love and Logic Solutions for Kids with Special Needs*, and coauthor, with Jim Fay, of *Teaching with Love and Logic*.